Preacher with a Billy Club

Preacher with a Billy Club

by

ROBERT C. ASMUTH

LOGOS, INTERNATIONAL
Plainfield, New Jersey

To the devoted and courageous members of the Fort Myers and Lake Park, Florida, Police Departments, with whom it has been my personal pleasure to serve.

Standard Book Number: 912106–18–2
Library of Congress Catalog Card Number: 76–154969
Logos, International, Plainfield, N.J. 07060

Printed in the United States of America

TABLE OF CONTENTS

The incidents related in this book are true. The names of persons, time sequences, and places have been changed to protect the innocent (and in some cases, the guilty).

PREFACE

God still works in mysterious ways, speaking through the Holy Spirit and touching men's lives! *Preacher with a Billy Club* was conceived by the Spirit of God. It all began because someone cared about me, about what I was doing, and took a personal interest in the work. A longtime personal friend, Patrick Kelly, a staff writer for the *Miami Herald* and formerly with the *Fort Myers News Press,* started it all with a front-page feature story on Palm Sunday two years ago. Interest in the work of a police chaplain aroused the curiosity of the Associated Press who sent a staff writer, Eric Sharp, from the Tampa Bureau to conduct an afternoon-evening-all-night on-the-scene action interview. The work became the subject of a wire story covering the nation from north to south and east to west. The uniqueness of this type of ministry stirred the creative imagination of Dan Malachuk of Logos International, and the straightforward approach from him was, "Would you consider writing a book about your experiences in law enforcement?"

But how does one write a book—write a book when you have never written anything longer than a college term paper or a Greek exegesis?! It's awesome. It's frightening! It's humbling! You pray, you write and rewrite, and completely commit the destiny of the undertaking to God. There's just no other way.

It has come alive now through the prodding and leading of the Holy Spirit and the prayers of a multitude of people.

My family, my friends, my deeply loved and respected congregation, my fellow law enforcement officers, and an entire community have been praying for me and *Preacher with a Billy Club*. I have felt the impact of these prayers and know they were there. Perhaps God in His continuing but mysterious workings and ways will speak through the pages of this book. Speak, because here is a valid and meaningful ministry. It is a ministry that has yet to be fully explored, one that has unlimited possibilities for creative and meaningful service to those who "hurt" in any number of ways.

The stories shared upon these pages are all true—I was there! Many never appeared on the "blotter" and even fewer were mentioned by the news media. Some, I know, sound incredible, unbelievable, and unreal. Some people will even react and say, "This just couldn't happen in my town!" Yet it did and it does! Tragically, it will continue until the Kingdom of God comes on earth as it is in heaven.

My greatest single mainstay during the laborious weeks and months of writing was my wonderful wife, Violet. She offered suggestions, assisted with the editing, and spoke encouraging words. Her prayers and encouragement saved the project from being aborted more than once. Her endless patience with, and understanding of, a temperamental novice author could come only because of her deep-seated belief in the book, an understanding of the task, and a faith in the worthwhileness of this particular ministry. My ever-present critics who eagerly awaited the completion of another chapter were my two teenaged sons, John and Paul. My nine-year-old, Cindy Sue, has been and still is excited about "my daddy's book." Another great person who stood staunchly by my side from beginning to end was my committed Christian secretary, Diane Nichols. She offered helpful editorial suggestions, typed and retyped manuscripts, and was devoted and dedicated to the entire project. She lived and breathed this book until it was finished. My friend Jamie Buckingham provided the finishing touches to the manuscript, tightening up lines, and sharing his feelings and insights for an action story such as this. Picture credits go to Joe Warner, a former law enforcement friend and presently staff photographer with the *Fort Myers News Press*.

My reward will be in seeing others respond to the challenge that is found in this type of ministry. Believing as I do that God still speaks, my prayer is that He will use *Preacher with a Billy Club* to speak to you.

Prologue

The sound of four gunshots broke the silence of the night, and a drunken migrant farm worker slumped to the ground in a dimly lit alley. . . . Suicide Annie is at it again, tenderly jabbing a butcher knife at her jugular vein knowing she'll be rescued before she's in danger. . . . A thirty-three-year-old woman abandons her children; then, in bare feet, short shorts, and tiny halter, appeals to the desk sergeant for help before turning abruptly and running to the top of the high bridge, planning to jump. . . . Two teenaged boys, victims of LSD (the hallucinogenic drug), have freaked out on trips. . . . A cracker-box dwelling suddenly becomes a mass of flames and you hear hysterical screams for help and the smell of burning flesh. . . . Distraught parents report their fourteen-year-old daughter has run away from home again. . . . A barroom brawl erupts and you find badly bleeding human beings half-dead on the sidewalk as you are surrounded by an angered mob of anti-police drunks. . . . An obviously pregnant and very disturbed unwed mother wields a pistol threatening her life, her angry lover, and three children. . . . Two naked drunks, one cut and profusely bleeding, the other brandishing a knife, barricade the door to a shack in an attempt to avoid arrest and medical treatment. . . . A jealous and jilted husband lays a gun on the desk and sobbingly confesses he almost killed two people in a fit of temper. . . . And, there's more! There's much more!

It's all part of the game of being a police chaplain. It's all part of a dirty night's work. It's a dirty job where you witness the indignities that one human being can inflict upon another. It's a dirty job where you witness man's inhumanity to man. The most tragic part is what man does to himself!

Somewhere someone has failed. Perhaps it was me. Perhaps it was you. Maybe it was both of us. Maybe it was and is the corporate and collective failure of the Church to fulfill its God-given ministry to mankind. Time, and time alone, will tell.

I. WHERE'S SAMMY?

Be not among winebibbers . . . (Prov. 23:20).

This was destined to be a typical Friday night! Oh, they are not all as bad as this one, but this one had had plenty of activity so far, and it was a long way from being over. It was May. Warm. Muggy. Full moon. The police blotter, for some unexplainable reason, is considerably larger when the moon is full than at other times. It's a bigger blotter still when the full moon comes on Friday—payday. Tonight was no exception.

"Fort Myers to cars four, seven, and eleven," crackled the voice of the dispatcher at the station.

The cars answered in sequence, giving their locations.

Again the dispatcher's voice: "Cars four, seven, and eleven.

Go to the Jolly Roger Bar; they've got a disturbance—a bad one. A man lying on the sidewalk. They think he's dead. Ambulance on the way."

Our car, car four, along with the others, acknowledged receipt of the complaint and headed to the scene of another barroom brawl. I was sitting in the front seat beside the lieutenant. He flicked on our red light, triggered the siren, and moved quickly through the streets of the tropical city to the trouble spot.

How many times, I thought, *have I been in a barroom brawl?* Sometimes we just pick up the broken pieces on our arrival. Then again we have to calm a few hotheads with too much "fightin' whiskey" in their systems. Quite frequently the scene is deserted upon our arrival. Many's the time, though, that we've loaded the squad cars with the drunken warriors, making them guests of the city for a night or several days.

A thousand thoughts raced through my mind as the siren wailed and the flashing red light made eerie reflections on the plate-glass windows along the way. *Where has society failed with these people? What causes the excessive drinking that results in a brawl? What could the Church have done that might have given these people's lives greater meaning than they could find at the bottom of an empty glass?*

With red lights flashing and sirens wailing, the three cars, one by one, arrived almost simultaneously at the scene. This one—I could tell—was going to be different. There were three fire trucks on the street ahead of us—but no fire. I could see a throng of milling, angry, drunken people all over the place.

"Barroom brawl," the dispatcher had said. To me it looked more like a riot!

The lieutenant turned to me: "Grab your billy club, and please, BE CAREFUL."

My billy club was clenched tightly in one hand, my flashlight in the other. The lieutenant was trotting toward the snarling mob, and I was directly behind him—I mean *directly* behind! I've always clung tenaciously to the theory that it's better to be a live coward than a dead hero. The way this gang was carrying on, any one of us might be a target for their vengeance.

I knew, as I approached the crowd, that this was not an ice-cream social or a Sunday school picnic! The big question was how to bring some reasonable degree of order out of this drunken chaos.

Heads were popping out of hotel windows and doorways. The usual assortment of sidewalk superintendents was engaged in its favorite nighttime spectator sport of watching the policemen separate the "good guys" from the "bad guys."

The firemen who had responded to the alarm were still trying to locate the nonexistent fire. Someone had called the police department, someone else the sheriff, another the ambulance, and still another had broken the glass in the alarm box and summoned the fire department. They had help—lots of it—whether they wanted help or not. Typically, although they had been quick to call for help, they were totally uncooperative upon our arrival.

Fortunately, the Jolly Roger Bar was completely empty except for the Mistletoe Rock Group that was still blaring away inside. Through the open door I could see into the dimly lit lounge that minutes before must have been overcrowded. Now it looked like a topsy-turvy disaster area. All the action was on the street and sidewalks in the immediate area. At least we wouldn't have to dodge flying chairs, tables, and bottles.

The air had the sickening aroma of a brewery. I could hear cries in the night:

"That man has a gun!"

"Watch out for Happy Harry! He's got a couple of big

knives!" But glancing here and there as we moved slowly through the crowd I still had not seen a sign of a single weapon.

Suddenly I heard shrieks from a hysterical woman: "He's dead! He's dead! They've killed my Sammy!" I began working my way through the crowd in the direction of the shrill voice.

The uniformed men had a couple of the more obviously intoxicated members of the group in frisking position at the side of the squad car, ready to load them in the back end. Another officer was dragging a lippy drunk to his cruiser.

"Fascist pig!" the man shouted. "Dirty, lousy, fuzz!"

"That's right, old buddy," the patient but determined officer replied. "I'm a fascist pig and a dirty, lousy, fuzz, but you're still going to jail."

The pleading cry of the woman rose again above the din: "Won't somebody please do something? Sammy is dead! Sammy! Oh God, my Sammy, he's dead."

I felt someone grab my arm. It was an attractive young girl in her early twenties—drunk.

"Reverend Asmuth," she said, "what are you doing here?"

She was one of my church members. Her presence at this barroom brawl was not going to contribute to harmony in her home, which was already on the rocks.

"Never mind what I'm doing here," I was tempted to say, "why aren't *you* home taking care of your children and husband?" But I held my tongue. This wasn't the moment nor the place for marital counseling. Edging away, I could hear her tell her cronies, "That's *my* minister!"

I was still trying to find Sammy.

"Over here—on the sidewalk—beside the gutter," called a frantic girl rushing toward me.

She knew who I was. They all knew who I was. My black shirt with its highly starched white clerical collar was a dead giveaway. So were my gold chaplain's badge and sleeve patches saying "City of Fort Myers Police."

"Father," she cried, tugging at my arm, "he's over here! He's dead—Sammy's dead. Please, Father, do something! Maria is about out of her mind." She was staggering as she led the way, clutching a glass containing the last few remaining sips of a cocktail.

Sammy was there all right, lying half on the sidewalk and half in the gutter. His wife Maria was hovering vulturelike over him. Deep sobs shook her slender body as she embraced him tightly. Her hands were covered with blood as was the sidewalk around them.

I knelt at her side and with my arm around her, whispered, "Maria, I'm Reverend Asmuth, the police chaplain. Perhaps I can help."

She raised her head ever so slightly, looked at me with big black eyes, and sobbing almost uncontrollably said, "Sammy's dead, Reverend. He's dead. He died in my arms."

Maria was a pretty girl, but her mascara was running wildly in all directions over a tearstained face. She was jerking spasmodically as she clung desperately to Sammy. I hooked my nightstick through my belt. Gently, I pulled her away from the body in the gutter. I motioned to her friend to help her, and asked someone else in the crowd to get a wet towel from the bar.

I looked down at the twenty-five-year-old body covered with blood, clothes torn half off. Blood was running profusely, obscuring his features. The curly blond hair lay tangled in vivid contrast to the red.

How many times had I seen heartache and ruin from the bottle? Marriages destroyed, innocent people dead, knifings, shootings, and fistfights just because people can't control their drinking! America's number-one drug problem is still alcohol!

Ten million known alcoholics, and the number is growing by the thousands each week.

When will that ambulance arrive? I thought. Then, *Maybe we don't need it.*

I placed my index and middle fingers on the limp wrist of Sammy's left arm, trying to find a pulse while I wiped blood from his face with the wet towel.

After what seemed an eternity, my searching fingers touched a faintly beating pulse. I turned to Maria: "Sammy might make it—he's still alive," I said.

"Thank God!" she screamed.

The ambulance screeched to a halt and the white-starched attendants wheeled the stretcher over toward us. They tied compresses over Sammy's wounds, gently lifted him onto the stretcher, and shoved it in the ambulance.

"Ride with him," I said to Maria, patting her shoulder. "I'll stop by the hospital and check with you later in the evening."

I knew the doctors would be busy when Sammy arrived at the emergency room. He was cut over both eyes, and his right eyelid had been laid back and damaged considerably. There was a five-inch gash down the inside of his left arm, and he had been stabbed deep in the pit of the stomach. He'd be scarred for life, but maybe he'd learned a lesson.

What next? I thought to myself. I moved toward a group gathered around a car parked near the bar. Sitting on the hood of the car was a heavyset man who had been wounded.

"Good buddy, how badly are you hurt? Let's take a look."

He lifted his shirt to show me where his stomach had been peeled back, and then showed me another wound on his arm. Both were deep. He needed medical attention. But he didn't want to go to the hospital in an ambulance.

"Will you let some of your friends take you?" I asked.

"Yeah, I guess so—in a little while," he said reluctantly.

I couldn't make him go, but those wounds needed to be

sewed up. Someone handed me one of the knives used in the foray—a rusty, dull hawkbill. It's one thing to be cut by a sharp blade. But a dirty, rusty, dull, hooked blade? No wonder Sammy was so badly torn up. He'd need a tetanus shot too.

We found the other knife and confiscated both of them. Since we had not actually seen the fight, we didn't make any arrests. Either man could have sworn out a warrant against the other, but neither ever did!

The Jolly Roger was back to business as usual. The barmaids and management had straightened up the inside while the drunks were outside. The Mistletoe Rock Group was in great form, several decibels louder than before. They had over two hours to go before the 2:00 A.M. closing.

Driving away from the scene, I radioed the station dispatcher that we were back in service.

"You reckon we should drive out to the hospital and check on your boy, Sammy?" the lieutenant asked.

"Tell you what, Lieutenant," I said, relaxing in the seat beside him. "I was at the station at 7:30 A.M. It's been a long day, and I'm hungry! Let's get some chow before they find something else for us to do."

Before the night was over we might even be back at the Jolly Roger. Some grilled cheese, potato chips, coffee, and pie were part of the ammunition needed to keep me going.

I had been awakened at seven that morning by the raucous ringing of the phone beside my bed.

It was Bill's aunt. She was calling from the police station. I had never met the aunt, but Bill was a familiar name and face to me. He had a lengthy arrest record at our station. Many seasoned criminals didn't have the number of arrests on their records that Billy did. He was a teenaged alcoholic, and this time he was charged on three counts: drunk, disorderly conduct, and resisting arrest without violence. His aunt's plea was simple: "Reverend Asmuth, Billy's in big trouble and needs your help. Will you come down to the station and try to do something?"

"Mrs. George, I can't make any promises," I told her. "It depends on Billy's attitude, and what we can work out through the court. I'll come on down and see what can be done, though."

I placed the phone in the cradle, silently thinking to myself, *Can he be helped? If he's convicted in court on all three charges, he'll draw about sixty five days. All this will do is dry him out until he can hit the nearest tavern. But how many times do you try to help a man? Seventy times seven? Well, I still have a long way to go then, if this is the case.*

I arrived at the station, exchanged greetings with the fellows in the squad room, the girls in records, and Ruth, the chief's redheaded secretary.

"Good mornin', Preach," the desk sergeant said cheerfully. "Sorry to bother you so early, but at least the eleven-to-seven shift didn't get you out of the sack when they brought this boy in last night. Do you want to talk to him first, or would you rather talk to his aunt?" He scratched at his head with his pencil and wrinkled his forehead at me.

"I think I'd rather talk with Billy's aunt first," I decided. "We've got to establish our ground rules for the problem before us."

Mrs. George was sitting in the waiting area, a plump matron in her sixties nervously turning a button on her flowered housedress. I introduced myself and we walked back to the captain's office. She was gallantly fighting to hold back the tears.

"Preacher, my husband and I have raised Billy since he was three years old. His father walked out when he was a baby, and no one has ever seen or heard from him since the day he left. Billy was just too much for his mother to handle. She brought him to our house early one morning to spend the day, and we haven't seen her since. That was some fifteen years ago. Seems like nobody ever cared for Bill but us." She fumbled in her large handbag for a handkerchief and dabbed at her eyes.

"How far did Billy get in school?" I asked.

"Well, he never did too good in school," she admitted. "He dropped out in the eighth grade. He ain't never held a job. The best he's done is like diggin' ditches and on road gangs. Seems as when he gets a good job he gets drunk, lands in jail, and is fired—the same thing over and over. We don't know what to do." She flung out her hands in a gesture of hopelessness.

"Do you think Billy would be receptive to going to the Alcoholic Rehabilitation Center again for treatment?" I asked.

"He might," she said with a try-anything look.

"He's been there twice before," I said. "It depends now upon his willingness to cooperate, the availability of space at the center, and securing the permission of the judge. I frankly believe that he's guilty as charged. Perhaps the judge will suspend the sentence on the three charges if we can get Billy to agree to go to the center for treatment."

"I'm sure he'll go if you tell him," said Mrs. George, sounding more discouraged than ever. She knew that Billy's two previous stays at the center had not changed him.

I took her back to the waiting room and asked Sarge to have one of the "trustees" bring Billy in to the captain's office. A dirty, disheveled, dissipated young man with long sandy hair entered the room. I motioned to the empty chair and asked him to sit down. He stared at the floor, avoiding my eyes.

"Billy, you're in a little trouble and perhaps we can give you some help. It's going to depend mostly upon you and what you want to do, however."

"I'm not in a little trouble, Reverend; I'm in big trouble," Billy said. He was speaking so low I could hardly hear him. "I lost my cool last night, got drunk, caused a scene in the bar, and bad-mouthed the cops. Now I've lost another job 'cause I didn't show up at work this morning." He raised his arm to drag a dirty sleeve across his nose. "I ain't got no money to pay bond, and my aunt don't have none either. What am I gonna do, Reverend? I'm gonna end up on skid row. You've gotta help me! You've just gotta!"

"If we could work it out for you, would you go back to the Alcoholic Rehabilitation Center?" I asked.

He nodded, his eyes dropping back toward the floor.

"Promise me one thing, Bill. If you go to the center this time, you've got to stay and complete the treatment program." I made it sound like an order. "I don't want you to bust out before you've been fully exposed."

"Yessir. This time I'll stay the whole time, and I'll talk with the counselors after I'm dismissed." Billy began to sound eager to cooperate.

I had my doubts, but we had to keep trying. *Okay, Rev*, I thought, *let's give it another try.*

"Billy, I want you to look at me. When was the last time you prayed?"

He hesitated for a moment and then said, "I guess when I was a little kid—a long time ago."

"Well, son, you and I are going to pray now."

He bowed his head and I reached across the captain's desk and placed my hands on his. I prayed silently, then I said, "Lord, we've got a young child of Yours with a nasty problem, and he needs Your help. Let him know Your presence in his life. Be his Companion and Guide in the days ahead that he may be victorious and spend his days in Your love and service, for Jesus' sake. Amen."

I heard a feeble "Amen" from Billy, as he raised his head. Tears were streaming down his face. We shook hands.

"You've got to go back to the cellblock now, Billy," I explained, "but I'm hoping that before the day is over we can have you on your way to the Center."

That afternoon the sergeant asked me, "Do you think it will work, Rev? Remember he bombed out of the Center twice before. He may be back here again before you know it."

"I don't know, Sarge, I just don't know. But we've got nothing to lose in trying again, and a whale of a lot to gain if he follows through." I was praying that Billy would make it.

II. LORD, WHY ME?

Whom shall I send? . . . Here am I, send me (Isa. 6:8).

"Two eggs scrambled, bacon and grits, a grilled cheese on white," the waitress yelled to the short-order cook as she clipped her order to the wire and rang his little bell. Moments later she appeared at the counter with our coffee, then disappeared again.

I looked down at my watch. It was 12:15 A.M.

While we waited and sipped our coffee, the lieutenant turned to me saying, "Rev, how did a nice guy like you ever get mixed up with a bunch of policemen? You hear things never intended for a minister's ears, and see things that make even the calloused sick at his stomach. You run the risk, like the rest of us, of getting your guts blown out. Yet, every Friday here you are, riding and working with us. How come, Rev, how come?"

I had often wondered about it myself. For fifteen years I'd been riding police cars—listening and ministering to the screams and cries in the night. The easy chair in front of the television would be far safer—but not nearly as rewarding.

"It goes back a long time," I said, "maybe back to the time when I was in grade school thirty years ago."

As I thought about it, the pieces began to fall together. I had been taught as a small child that the policeman was my friend. He was more than a friend; he was almost an idol. I wanted to be a policeman when I grew up.

I remembered my years as a school-crossing guard, the pride I had when I wore that patrol belt and badge. Each June they called my name in assembly and the police department representative gave me another certificate for the year's service. I had many hours of service to my credit when I finished junior high school.

Officer Jensen was a real friend. He stood with us each day and helped us at the busy intersection. He was a giant of a man, his uniform clean and neatly pressed, his long blue winter coat with its shining brass buttons highly polished, and there was always a warm, compassionate smile on his face.

When I was a freshman in college God laid His hand on my shoulder and called me to the Gospel ministry: "Take the Word of God to a spiritually starved but unwilling world," He commanded.

My years of college and graduate school passed quickly and the dream of my high calling in Jesus Christ became a reality.

Following a brief two-year ministry in Cincinnati, Ohio, I accepted a nebulous challenge from a new church development in a growing suburb of West Palm Beach, Florida. I was to become a missionary.

Florida's population explosion in the fifties was demanding a host of new churches. My wife and I were young, filled with the spirit of adventure. We accepted the challenge of organizing a new church.

The four-acre site, selected by our denominational representatives, was located in an area surrounded by scrub pines that howled ferociously when the wind blew, palmetto bushes filled with king-sized diamondback rattlesnakes, billions of mosquitoes, and several miles of paved streets and sidewalks. But there were no houses and no people.

The streets and sidewalks had been put in just before the crash of '29, and little else had been done. The streets were now in bad need of repair, and the sidewalks—where you could find them—were covered with an abundance of weeds and sandspurs.

Who in their right mind would locate a church in this desolate wilderness? I thought to myself. Then, gathering every ounce of courage I could muster, I put the same question to the men from the New York office.

"*You* will," came the emphatic reply from the Board's representatives, more affectionately referred to as the men from "Heaven on the Hudson." "In just a few years you'll be sitting in the middle of the biggest housing development in the entire state of Florida."

As Thomas doubted, so did I. I played the role to the fullest. The first phase of the building program was completed, but there were still no signs of any human beings. The whole congregation had to drive to church. The words of the men from "Heaven on the Hudson" kept hounding me, but still no sign of the BIG housing development which was supposed to spring up magically around our isolated church building located in the no-man's-land miles away from civilization.

Late one night as I worked in the church office, a car pulled into the parking lot and the headlights hit the office windows. The lights went out, a door slammed, and I heard footsteps approaching the door. My heart almost stopped! Who would be out at this hour of the night? It took a bit of doing to find this place without a road map, but this car pulled right up, and someone was coming to the door.

Before I had a chance to respond to the knock, a big deep voice boomed out: "Reverend Asmuth, is that you in there?" Whoever it was at least knew my name.

"Yes, sir, I'm in here." I replied, a little nervously. "Who is it?"

"It's Lieutenant Michael Manning of the police department. Are you all right?"

What a relief! I dragged myself from the chair to the door to let my newly found friend in the building. The paleness of my face under a deep Florida tan was a dead giveaway to Mike. He was all apologies for having startled me, but said that he had seen the lights when he was just making a routine check of the building. We visited for a good while and had coffee together before he left.

This was the first of many visits Mike was to make, along with the other men of the department. It broke up the monotony on some long, lonely, and quiet nights for them, and gave me the reassurance that someone out there was concerned about me and would respond if I ever needed help.

One night Mike got a call about an attempted suicide while he was in the office having coffee with me.

"Maybe," said Mike, "you'd like to go along on this one. Your help might be of more value in this situation than mine."

I went that night—and many other nights. There seemed to be something uniquely effective in having a minister work with the police in some situations.

Then one day it happened. The office telephone rang. It was the chief of police. Again my heart did flip-flops. *What did he want with me?* I couldn't think of any flagrant violation of the law that I had committed. *The chief, calling me? How come?*

"Would you," he asked, "consider being our police chaplain? The job doesn't pay any salary, would be strictly voluntary, and you'd be subject to call when we needed you. If you could, the men would like to have you ride with them when you have some spare time. It would help me, help the Department, and add some stature and dignity to law enforcement."

Flattery will get you everywhere, I thought, and I accepted immediately, beginning many pleasant years of experience with the Lake Park Police Department. And it all began because that "friendly policeman"—remembered since early childhood—became concerned about "Rev" working late at night in a church that sat in the wilderness.

Later years revealed the wisdom of my New York friends in choosing the location. It did become a sprawling housing development, with the church building strategically placed right in the middle!

Eight years ago God called me again, this time to a pastorate in Fort Myers, Florida. Fort Myers is a Gulf Coast city of 30,000, a hub in a growing county of over 100,000, the population of which almost doubles during the height of the winter season.

I sat quite innocently one morning in a ministerial association meeting. I didn't usually attend such meetings, but something had compelled me to go that morning. In the routine business, the president shared a communication from the chief of police, Burl A. Underhill. It was an appeal for help. He was looking for a chaplain who would work with his department. It was a volunteer job for a man to assist with the personal problems of his officers, provide counsel—when requested—to the inmates of the city jail, and help with the broad area of "public service."

There was absolute silence. My mind whirled under the pressure of the necessity for a quick decision. I had enjoyed the work in Lake Park, but I wasn't sure that I wanted to start riding in police cars again, risking my life, and having to listen to obscenities for hours on end. After all, there are other ways you can serve your community as a minister that don't have the same sort of built-in risk factors.

Then there was my new congregation. Larger and more conservative, would they be patient if I had to break an occasional appointment when an emergency situation arose? Knowing the places I'd be asked to go, I wondered if I could make the church members understand.

My family was sure to have their doubts, too. When our children were little, they were thrilled that I could ride in police cars. But now that they were getting older, would they resent the hours added to an already busy schedule that would keep me away from home? I knew my wife wouldn't argue with the idea, but she would certainly be entitled to a pained, "Here we go again" expression.

Yet it's the sort of thing that gets in your blood and becomes a part of your being. Police work had become part of my total character. I knew I was hooked!

The Holy Spirit prodded me, and I raised my hand. A new chapter in my life was about to unfold. I would be serving my community in an area where I truly believed that the Church should be represented, touching the lives of many people whom the Church had never touched. That's why I was where I was.

"You know, Lieutenant," I explained, "the Church's work isn't confined to those buildings of concrete and steel. The work of the Church is with people. It's with people who are in trouble—bad people, good people, mixed-up people, people from all walks of life, and people of all colors. As a police chaplain I feel I'm doing something that may be of value. If I can add one brick to the wall of human dignity through my efforts then it has been worthwhile."

The bell at the kitchen window rang, and our waitress returned with both hands laden with food.

I was hungrier than I thought, and before she left the counter I ordered another sandwich. The lieutenant shook his head. He just didn't understand how a skinny guy like me could stash the food away and still not get fat. Me, I never worried about it; I just kept on eating.

A few minutes later the waitress hurried to the counter. "Lieutenant, you're wanted on the telephone."

He strode to the telephone, listened intently, then came running back, grabbing his hat.

"Let's go!" he said.

"But my sandwich!" I protested.

"Forget it, Rev—let's go."

He was gunning the motor by the time I got to my side of the car. Coffee and sandwiches are fine, but everything is secondary when human lives are at stake. I could eat and sleep tomorrow. Tonight I was a policeman.

III. PEDRO'S PLIGHT

Let not your hearts be troubled . . . (John 14:1).

"Tell the dispatcher we're 10–8 and 10–51 (enroute to) Pango Drive," the lieutenant ordered. I pressed the mike button and relayed the message back to headquarters. Pango Drive is a substandard housing area where people live like animals in the crowded shacks.

The siren on the cruiser was wailing, and the red light was flashing. We were in a hurry.

"Bad house fire out there," the lieutenant said. "There may be two signal 7's (dead persons). Gorrell (the dispatcher) says the house will probably be total."

"You know, Loot," I said, remembering the ramshackle section, "if that fire gets out of control we may lose the whole of Pango Drive. Those houses are so close they'll burn like matchboxes."

I could see the flames as we approached the area, and felt the heat as we parked our vehicle near the property.

"Car four to Fort Myers. 10–97 Pango Drive," I said, as we killed the engine and grabbed our flashlights.

We joined the other uniformed officers who were conferring with the assistant fire chief. The blazing house had been occupied by two males, one female, and several children.

"We've evacuated all the victims from the house," the fireman said. "A teenaged boy went through that fiery furnace and gathered five children. They're okay, but an old man is badly burned as is a younger man. Both are on their way to the hospital. The woman is dead. We're waiting for the coroner now."

One dead, and the future of two others still unknown. I could smell the burned flesh. I walked over to where the body of the dead woman was lying on the ground covered with a white sheet. I gently pulled the sheet back. She was not badly burned. The fire chief joined me.

"Suffocation," he said. "We just couldn't get her out in time."

"How'd the fire start, Chief?" I inquired. I knew it was the wrong time of year for kerosene heaters, or an overload on inadequate electrical wiring in the dwellings.

"It was some kind of a love triangle," the chief said, shaking his head. "The old man and the other fellow were living with this woman. The old man wanted her and said that if he couldn't have her he would kill them all. Everyone had been drinking, and suddenly the old boy pulled his cigarette lighter out of his pocket and threw it into a pile of papers on the floor. You can take it from there. The whole thing just went poof! The boys have the fire pretty well under control now, and we'll be moving out in just a few minutes. Kinda sad, isn't it, Reverend," he said as he slowly walked away.

I nodded, at a loss for words. Then one of the uniformed officers came running up.

"Rev," he said, "the dispatcher said the hospital wants you to come right out. They're having quite a problem with one of the victims from this fire. He's hysterical and they think maybe you can help get him calmed down."

"Take our car, Rev," the lieutenant ordered. "I'll meet you later."

The emergency room was filled with the sickening stench of burned flesh. I walked past the first of several cubicles and saw my buddy, Sammy, moaning and groaning. The medical staff was still busy sewing up his many cuts.

A nurse motioned me to the next cubicle. There on the table was Carlos, the old man from the fire. His body was severely burned and he was in excruciating pain. He looked like a huge piece of raw meat. The nurse indicated the prognosis was not good. Carlos was critical—expected to die any minute.

"Your man," she said, "is in the next cubicle. His name is Pedro, and he's incoherent—keeps talking about a girl named Louisa, and asking for his children."

"Does he know Louisa died in the fire?" I asked.

"No, no one has told him. You're going to have to break that news to him somehow."

I was walking slowly, praying earnestly: "Lord, this is going to be a tough one. Give me what I need to help Pedro accept what has happened."

I knew I was going to need all the help I could get. Pedro's agonizing screams, a combination of Spanish and English, were half-understandable. He was going to get old Carlos for starting that fire. He was greatly concerned about the little children. And he kept calling for Louisa.

I was about to part the curtain and enter Pedro's cubicle when the nurse called me aside.

"Carlos just died," she said. "I thought you might want to know before you went in to see Pedro."

"Thanks a lot," I said. "Too bad about Carlos, but the way Pedro is carrying on in there he'd probably try and kill him anyway before the sun came up. Maybe we've been spared another murder."

Pedro saw me part the curtains and he sat up on the examining table.

"Padre, Padre!" he shouted.

"Yes, Pedro, I'm a padre!" I found myself saying to the man whose world I was going to dash to pieces in a few moments. "God," I prayed, "show me the right way to tell him."

Pedro slid from the table and embraced me, the way Spanish-American people are inclined to do. Then he began sobbing.

"I try be brave, Padre. Honest, I try be brave," he sobbed. "It was awful—flames everywhere, much smoke. I get out of house—I don't know how, but I get out. My children, I know not. Padre, my children, they are safe? Say yes, that they are safe, Padre." His dark eyes were full of pleading.

"Your children are all safe, Pedro," I said. "A teenaged boy got them out—saved their lives. They're staying with a neighbor."

He seemed relieved and reassured. Then his expression became pained as he grasped for his next sentence. Tears began to fill his eyes. Clenching my arms tightly he looked piercingly into my eyes so I couldn't escape him.

"Padre, my Louisa? What about my Louisa, Padre?"

Don't put it off, Rev, he's got to know. You can't keep it from him forever, an inner voice seemed to say. *But be gentle with it, Rev, be gentle!*

I tried to look at him straight.

"Pedro, Louisa wasn't as lucky as the children. She died—not from burns but from suffocation by smoke. They tried to reach her, but it was too late. The firemen gave mouth-to-mouth resuscitation to try to save her, but—I'm sorry, Pedro, but your Louisa has gone to be with God."

"Oh, my God, not my Louisa!" he screamed. "My Louisa can't die, she can't die." He raised his hands, imploring heaven, and then collapsed in a dead weight in my arms!

I held him and let him cry it out. Long minutes later he began to get control. I felt his body grow rigid with hatred.

"Carlos," he hissed with vengeance in his voice. "That dirty old Carlos. He did it. He killed my Louisa! I get Carlos and I kill him like he kill my Louisa. I kill him! I kill him! I kill him!"

"Look at me, Pedro," I said softly. "You will not kill Carlos. He did a bad thing in starting that fire, but you will not kill him. Carlos was burned terribly in the fire. He's already dead. He died just a few minutes ago in the next room."

All tension suddenly drained from him as he heaved a deep sigh. It was as if justice had been meted out. Forgiveness would be easier now.

"How do you feel, Pedro?" I inquired.

He was still sobbing, but less agonizingly. His conversation was becoming more intelligible as he sat upright on the examining table, his feet dangling over the side. The tranquilizer the hospital staff had given Pedro before I arrived was beginning to work. It was time to think now about taking him back to Pango Drive to retrieve his children. They would need their daddy.

"Pedro, do you feel up to leaving the hospital?" I encouraged. "The doctors say it's all right."

"Where you take me, Padre?" he asked, giving me a trusting look.

"I'm going to take you back to Pango Drive, so you can be with your children," I said. His face lit up. He placed both feet on the floor.

"Why we wait anymore, Padre?" he said. "Let's go. I want to see my children."

Pango Drive had calmed down. Most of the uniformed men were gone, with the exception of one officer and the lieutenant. Before us were the smoking ruins of Pedro's home.

"Do you know which neighbor would have your children?" I asked. He shook his head but strode confidently forward.

"Come this way, Padre. I show you who we ask about them," he said.

We walked down a dimly lit alley where all the shacks looked exactly alike to me. About a hundred yards from the highway he stopped.

"We go this way," he said; "it's this house here."

A single light was burning, casting an eerie shadow on the dirt path before us. There were no sounds from within. We knocked, and a feeble voice answered, "Come in, it's unlocked."

Within the single room structure we found a bed, the makings of a kitchen, one chair, and a television set. A little old lady, obviously suffering from a stroke, limped about behind a walker. She tried to be sympathetic and understanding, while Pedro tried his best to be a brave martyr, but neither could contain his grief, and the inevitable wailing session began. It became loud and emotional, and the only thing I could do was wait it out. Pedro finally asked the old woman about his children and I took advantage of the opportunity:

"Pedro, she's told us who is keeping your children. Let's go to them now," I said, taking him by the arm and leading him toward the door.

Suddenly I heard, "Mister Reverend, after you leaves Pedro I'se wants you to come back here if you will, please."

It was the old woman. I promised I'd be back as soon as I

could. Pedro and I walked together past several more shacks, coming upon one that was in total darkness.

"This is the place," he said confidently, nodding his head vigorously up and down.

"Pedro, are you sure?" I asked him. "There isn't a light on in the house." I didn't particularly like the idea of waking people unnecessarily in the middle of the night. But he was sure. We knocked. A little teenaged girl answered the door and invited us to enter.

Pedro received sympathy from his little friend, precipitating a new flood of tears. It was difficult not to become personally caught up in the trauma. I fought to keep from being involved, knowing that once I was, my effectiveness with them would be finished.

"Honey," Pedro said, addressing the young lady, "my children—where are they? Are they all right?"

She nodded, taking Pedro's hand and leading us to the doorway into another room. She cracked the door slightly, and my gaze caught the figures of five children all sleeping soundly on one big bed.

"Ah, they are hokay," a pleased Pedro said.

As I prepared to leave I turned to Pedro:

"This has been a tough night, my friend," I said, "and there are going to be some hard times ahead, days when living will be difficult for you. Perhaps, before I leave, you and your friend will join me in prayer. We need to call upon our God, seeking His strength and His peace in these heartbreaking experiences."

"I like, Padre. I like if you pray for me. And please—pray for my children and for my Louisa—may her soul rest in peace," Pedro stammered, his voice choked with emotion.

We joined hands and prayed together. Then I walked out into the trash-littered alley, trusting that I could find the first dwelling we had entered. I recognized a garishly painted garbage can I had noticed earlier and climbed up the steps to knock on the flimsy front door. A voice inside said, "Come in, Reverend, Sir." I found the old woman sitting in the same position as when I had left earlier.

"Reverend, Sir, may I ask a favor of you?" she asked.

"Yes, ma'am, you may ask a favor of me," I found myself saying, wondering what it would be.

"Well, Mister Preacher-Policeman" (that was something I'd never been called before), "would you be so kind as to get channel twenty on my television set?" she said simply.

I was stunned! She'd called me all the way back here for *that!*

"Yes, ma'am, I'd be happy to get channel twenty for you," I said, reaching down to adjust the dial. "Now before I leave is there anything else you need?" I asked. Surely, she hadn't wanted me to come back just for that.

"No, sir, not a thing," came the cheery reply. "Thank you again, and good night, Mister Preacher-Policeman."

What about that! I had a new name—"Mister Preacher-Policeman." I found myself chuckling as I walked down the dirt road toward the police cruisers. The lieutenant must have heard me as I came into view. I'm sure he thought I'd flipped —a guy who'd been working with death and grief, laughing to himself.

"Rev," he said as I came closer, "what in the world happened back there?" He stuck his head out the window of the cruiser to peer intently at me.

I shared my new name of "Mister Preacher-Policeman," and the old "loot" doubled up with laughter. It was a name destined to stick.

We checked back in service with the dispatcher.

"Fort Myers to car four, 10–19 (return to station) and answer some of these complaints," the voice said.

At least, I thought, *you can't get into too much trouble at the station answering complaints.* Six blocks away from the station the lieutenant turned to me.

"Say, Rev," he said, "will you ever forget our near riot several months ago? The troops are still circulating stories that you had more than a billy club when you jumped out of the car that night. S'pose they'll ever learn the whole truth about that one?" He looked at me and chuckled. I grinned back at him, thinking about my un-chaplainlike role that night.

It was near the end of a long hot summer, and the county was sitting on a racial keg of dynamite. Every situation was tense and had the makings of a full-scale riot. But we had been lucky. We always managed to snip the fuse just in the nick of time, and fortunately no one got hurt, nor had there been any serious consequences.

Then one night at the shopping center all hell broke loose. It was a night I'll remember forever.

IV. NO RIOT TONIGHT, BOYS!

Come now, let us reason together, says the Lord (Isa. 1:18).

Our town has always taken pride in its relations between the races. We've tried to understand each other, and while our progress might be slower than in some other sections of the country, still we've been able to report progress. This hasn't made everyone happy, but it has helped keep the peace in the community. Sometimes it's better to be dragging your heels and having things go smoothly than to go rushing right into it, suffering a series of bad reactions. But unfortunately, things weren't going fast enough for some in the Negro community, and much too fast for some in the white community. It was bound to come to a head.

The unrest grew. Like all members of the department I was on the standby list, not making a move without reporting my destination and how I could be reached to the desk sergeant.

Every police department has personnel problems during the summer months. There are only so many weeks to squeeze in vacations, and the men with children wanted their time off while the kids were out of school. This handicapped our department. We had only fifty-six men, including the officers with rank, the patrolmen, and the plainclothes division. Divided into three shifts, allowing for days off and vacations, we had very few men in action at any given time.

My family had gone to Chicago to visit my wife's parents. This left me with free time after I left the church in the late afternoon, and permitted me to spend several hours an evening riding with the men. As the summer progressed, the racial tension built to a fever pitch.

Night after night I rode the cars, feeling more like a community public-relations man for the police department than a chaplain. I'd smile, wave, speak, and do whatever I could to ease the tension. We backed up every car that answered a complaint in a potential trouble spot. While I was uneasy, I made it a point to get out of the car and mingle with the people because I knew it wouldn't take much to start full-scale trouble.

Riots never solve anything. Someone always gets hurt—usually innocent people—property is destroyed, and in the end the antagonism is worse than ever. Seldom, if ever, is anything accomplished when men revert to acts of violence.

One night we answered a call to a minor automobile accident in the black community. It wasn't anything serious, but there was the usual confusion, and crowds began to gather. Everyone was quite good-natured and in a good frame of mind. The wreckers hauled the cars away, the street was cleaned up, and we started to leave.

Just then a couple of drunks came tumbling out of a bar arguing with each other. We heard the noise and turned just in time to see one swing at the other. Luckily there was another car with us, and we moved in to separate the fighters.

Suddenly, without any warning, we were surrounded by swarms of angry blacks. They were yelling and shouting, egging these two guys on. We knew we had to stop the fight—quick—without hurting either of the drunks. A white billy club across a black scalp would have instantaneously started a full-scale riot.

The spectators didn't want the fight interrupted. But this was no time to be patient. We took the fighters by surprise, pinned their arms to their sides, and the fight was over! The lieutenant and I took one man, the other two officers the second fellow. We shoved them in the "wire cage" in the back seats of the two patrol cars and the lieutenant said, "Let's go."

There were a few obscenities as we wheeled away and someone called us "stinking white honkies," but we were clear. On our way into the station we asked the dispatcher to send another car to drive through the area to make certain the crowd had dispersed.

Our "passenger" couldn't remember who started the fight, nor did he remember what they were fighting about. He was downright apologetic for his behavior and resigned to the fact he was going to spend the next six hours, at least, in the drunk tank. Things remained quiet in the black community the rest of the night, however.

As the summer wore on, there were other minor skirmishes, each worse than the one before as the heat and humidity became more intense. Carloads of white youths began driving through the black community, heckling, throwing things, and then speeding away. The black youths were playing the same kind of game.

Typical of the animosity was an incident that took place late one night. Two young black boys were hitchhiking through town enroute to the east coast. Their ride had dropped them off, and they were standing alongside the highway, trying for another. A truckload of white boys passed them, calling out some filthy names. The truck circled the block and the boys continued the name-calling. The black boys responded this time—cursing back. The truck stopped and they went at it. The Negro youths were outnumbered three to one and never had a chance.

A passing motorist hailed us and told us where the fracas was taking place. We headed for the scene, and when we came into view the truck with its passengers peeled rubber and went flying off. The bleeding black boys had nowhere to go.

We didn't know whether we should chase the truck or help the boys, but it seemed wiser to stop. We radioed a description of the truck, while we did what we could to help the hitchhikers. With cooperation from the sheriff's departments in the two neighboring counties, we were able to get the boys rides to their homes on the east coast.

One thing became apparent, however. Had this been a full-scale riot we would not have been equipped to handle it. Our car's riot equipment was of pre-World War II vintage. The tear-gas bombs all had expiration dates that made them products of antiquity. We were short on hard hats, riot guns, and most of the necessary equipment for subduing a riot with weapons. We dreaded facing the time when our weapons would be pressed into use.

The summer approached mid-August, and everyone was convinced we were going to have a riot. The town was rampant with rumors as to where it would start and at what time. Everyone in town seemed to be an authority on riots. People were buying up weapons and ammunition at the sporting-goods stores as if they were going out of style. Some places were completely sold out.

I left the station with the lieutenant on a Tuesday night in mid-August. He was good and upset. No men! Days off and vacations had reduced the available manpower to one car with a black officer, two cars with white officers, the lieutenant and myself. It wasn't very comforting. If anything did happen, we'd make a pretty poor showing.

The lieutenant's intuition told him something big was going to happen that night. We kept busy on small things, however, answering complaints, making arrests, and backing up the other three cars that were on the road. Then the radio crackled into life again, with an urgency that spelled trouble!

"Fort Myers to cars four, seven, nine, and fourteen," the dispatcher said. Without waiting for any of us to answer he proceeded: "Big fight at shopping center on Oak Street. It's a racial disturbance."

All cars acknowledged the call. We were the closest, only a block-and-a-half away. Our tires squealed, the red light came on, and the siren blared. In the car there was stony silence. Neither of us said a thing for what seemed like an eternity. Then the lieutenant turned to me and with machine-gun rapidity gave me my instructions:

"When we get there, Rev, you grab the shotgun and corral the colored kids. I'll get the whites. Just get them off to one side of the lot, away from the other boys."

This was the thing we had all dreaded. I knew the other cars were on the way, but it was going to take them several minutes to give us the backing we needed. Until then, the lieutenant and I had it all by ourselves. We wheeled into the parking lot, stopped, and jumped out.

"This is it, Rev," he said. "Be mighty damn careful that you don't get yourself hurt."

One look at that milling gang and I was ready to raise the white flag. There were at least 150 of them, ranging in age from fourteen to twenty-one—half black, half white. All were stripped to the waist, and I spotted weapons of every description! Guns of assorted calibers, chains, brass knuckles, wide belts wrapped about fists, zip guns, slingshots, and broken bottles. This gang hadn't come together to play scrabble!

The lieutenant went toward his mob and I headed toward mine.

"Okay, boys, back up," I heard him say with authority. His group obeyed, but mine didn't. They came toward me savagely, brandishing their weapons.

Clutching my shotgun, I mustered up my best preaching voice and with a pulpit sound that had often struck out at sin I barked out a command:

"You heard the lieutenant! Back up! I want you all off over there." I swung the gun barrel in the direction I wanted them to go.

A large boy with muscles rippling under his black skin moved toward me, swinging a length of chain in his hand. His eyes glittered.

"I've walked into one of those guns before, cop," he said. "You're not gonna scare me." Then he must have spotted my clerical collar. "Look guys," he boomed, "this one ain't even a cop—he's a preacher or somethin' like that."

"Bet he don't even know how to shoot a gun," another taunted, advancing toward me. I didn't dare show how uncourageous I felt just then.

"Keep walking if you want to, son," I said, "but if you want to stay healthy, you best get back into the corner of that lot. I mean it!" I used a calm but ferocious tone of voice as I pumped a shell into the chamber of the gun. The hollow sound of the shotgun shell moving into the barrel did it. He moved—backward!

Their authority was broken, and the groups began to disperse. It was hard to tell if they were deserting the cause or going to find reinforcements. We needed reinforcements too. I was hoping and praying they were on their way.

The other three cars arrived almost immediately. We moved through the mob, disarming those with weapons. Things were cooling off.

The sound of the dispatcher's voice on the car radio caught my attention. One of the men answered and brought us the message:

"Captain House is at the station, and he wants us to bring in all the boys involved."

All the boys? I groaned. *Impossible!* However, that was the captain's order, and it had to be followed. We'd already lost about two-thirds of them anyway. Yet how do you put even fifty boys into four police cars? Some of them had their own transportation, so we had to risk letting them use it. It looked like a troop convoy going down the busy thoroughfares at 2:00 A.M. as we took the remnants of our group to the station.

We interrogated the boys one by one until dawn. The station house isn't very large, and we had to find four separate areas for questioning. We had to keep the white and black boys separated; then we had to separate those we had questioned from those we hadn't. All agreed on one point—the major issue in the disturbance was race. A white boy had made a degrading remark to one of the black boys a few days earlier. Harsh words, then threats, had been exchanged, and finally: "You bring your gang, and I'll bring mine," they had agreed.

The captain, the lieutenant, and I sat and patiently listened to their stories until dawn. Then the three of us conferred. It was agreed that the less said about the incident, the better. There would be no arrests made and no charges filed.

We walked from the smoke-filled office to the smoke-filled lobby. All the boys were brought before us. We tried to impress upon them the seriousness of what had nearly happened.

We didn't threaten any of the boys. They had not been abused, and we told them that no arrests would be made nor would their names be entered on the log. Then we made them all shake hands with each other before leaving.

The boys were all looking sheepish, and some were even smiling as they shook hands. Suddenly one of the boys began to shout and curse:

"I'm not shaking hands with any stinking nigger."

I could feel my stomach tie up in knots. I looked at the boy and my mouth went dry. He was one of my own church members. One of the officers yanked him out of the room, and we told him in pretty blunt language that he was on the verge of going to jail. I tried to cram back into his head some of the Christianity he'd forgotten somewhere along the line. I offered no sympathy. He could either go apologize to the boy, and shake hands, or spend the night behind the bars. He chose to apologize, and we finally dismissed them.

The town, for the most part, didn't even know what had happened. And it was just as well. The less said about some of these things the better. The problem was settled without violence and without anyone suffering any bodily injury. We went the rest of the summer without trouble. I didn't have to "ride shotgun" again.

V. DON'T JUMP

Who shall separate us from the love of Christ? (Rom. 8:35).

The lieutenant and I were in his office. It was almost midnight and we were filing record cards. I faintly heard the desk sergeant saying to someone who had come in off the street, "Yes, ma'am, may I help you?"

"If you won't help me," a woman screamed, "I'll jump off that bridge!"

I got up from my chair in time to see a barefooted young woman in short shorts and a bikini halter glaring at the sergeant. Her feet were filthy and her black hair a tangled mass.

"I've already been to the Salvation Army," she shouted, "and they were all going home and told me to come back tomorrow! All the churches are locked, and if you don't help me there's no sense in me living!"

"I'm sorry, ma'am, but all we've got is the jail," the sergeant said apologetically.

Suddenly she turned and darted out the door, turning toward the seventy-foot-high bridge that spans the Caloosahatchee River—a bridge where pedestrians are prohibited.

"Lieutenant! Reverend! She's getting away! We've got to catch her before she jumps!" Sarge hollered as he went charging out the front door of the station, his keys jangling.

The lieutenant and I bolted through the front door behind him after I flung a message over my shoulder to the radio dispatcher:

"Better dispatch one of the downtown cars to the approach of the bridge. We might not catch her."

"Will do, Rev," he said, as I went dashing out in the direction of the chase.

She had a good start on us and was out of sight as I cut across the front lawn toward the bridge approach. The sergeant and lieutenant were several paces ahead of me, running for all they were worth. I hoped that the squad car would be along soon and head her off before it was too late.

The police car, its rotating light cutting a path of brilliant red through the darkness of the night, was coming up behind us—fast. My pace and that of my running partners slowed to a trot as I tried to catch my breath. The cruiser squealed to a stop just ahead of the frantically running woman.

The girl had not yet reached the top of the bridge, and the quick-thinking officer tried to head her off. She was apparently going to try to get to the top of the bridge railing and jump.

The officer reached her, and with a lunge tackled her around the midsection. The two of them fell backward, the officer landing on his hind side on the concrete, followed by the angry young woman on top of him. She was waving arms, kicking legs, and putting up a good struggle.

"Let me go!" she screamed. "Lemme go! You ain't gonna stop me! I wanna die. If I wanna die no pig like you is gonna stop me! Lemme go!"

"Let's get this woman into the car and take her back to the station," the lieutenant said, grabbing her arms and pinning them behind her.

She didn't want to go. She really hadn't broken any law, so they couldn't arrest her. But if she persisted much longer with her foul language she would be charged with causing a disturbance. She managed to get in a few scratches and kicks in the shins before we had her settled in the back seat of the cruiser.

The lieutenant asked the sergeant to ride in the cruiser with the patrolman and the woman. Then he and I walked back.

"Loot," I asked, "just what do you plan on doing with that little lady when they get her to the station? We can't book her and put her in jail, you know."

"She's going to be your problem, Rev," he said, smiling. I was afraid of that.

The desk sergeant told us that the would-be bridge jumper was in the lieutenant's office with the patrolman. He didn't have to tell us, we could hear her. I took a deep breath and walked in.

"Young lady," I said, "I don't know who you are or why you wanted to jump from that bridge a few minutes ago. I do know that I'd like to try to help you if I can. The problem might have been bigger than you, and bigger than me, but it's not bigger than God." I watched her to see how she would take my opening attempt to reach her.

She only glared at me. She did not want to talk! There was fire in her eyes, and a determined expression on her face. It looked like the next move was up to me.

"Where are you from?" I asked.

"Fort Walton Beach," came the crisp reply, her eyes fixed on the floor.

"Fort Walton Beach!" I exclaimed, knowing that was far from Fort Myers. "Where are you headed?"

She fired back her reply: "Here."

"Do you have kinfolk here?" I was trying to find some help for her.

"No, no one. I just wanted to come to Fort Myers." She was beginning to warm up.

"Just wanted to come to Fort Myers," I mused aloud. Then I asked, "Are you married?"

"No, I'm divorced. My husband left me about five years ago."

"Do you have any children?"

"Four," she said as a slow smile spread across her face. "Want to see their pictures?" She rummaged through her purse, then handed me four wallet-size photos. "This is Beth, she's five; this is Tommy who's seven; and Jamie who's eight; and Karen who's eleven."

"And what's your name?" I asked.

"I'm Gloria, and I'm thirty-three," she said.

"Where are your children?"

"They're back in Fort Walton Beach."

"Who's taking care of them?"

"Oh, they're with a neighbor. At least that's where they were when I left this morning." She sounded a little uneasy about them.

This thing just wasn't making good sense. The only time she'd looked me in the eye was when I asked her about her children, yet it looked as if she'd abandoned them. There had to be something behind it.

"Look, Gloria, I want to help you if I can," I said. "But you've got to level with me. You start shooting square, and I'll do what I can. Don't make me pick it out of you, piece by piece."

At this her eyes welled up with tears, and she shook with heavy sobs. As she regained control of herself she began:

"My husband left me right after our youngest was born. He had a good job, and we enjoyed the nicer things of life. But when he left, he left for good. That was five years ago, and I don't even know where he is." She started crying again and I handed her my handkerchief. "I lost the house because I couldn't make the payments. The finance company repossessed the car. We're living in a small trailer and I've jumped from job to job until I've just about had it." She shrugged her shoulders at the hopelessness of it all.

"There's another man in your life, isn't there, Gloria?" I ventured, knowing there had to be a reason for her actions. "This is the real reason you've come to Fort Myers, isn't it?"

She dropped her eyes to the floor as she whispered, "How'd you know, Reverend? How'd you know?"

"Just a hunch, Gloria," I replied, honestly, "just a hunch."

Bit by bit she told me the rest of it. Gloria was a woman with two years of college who had flunked out in marriage and now was about to lose her children. She pinned her only hope for happiness on a married man who encouraged her love even though he said marriage was impossible. Grasping for straws, she had chased him from city to city until she wound up in Fort Myers. And now she had discovered he wasn't here anymore either.

"Gloria," I said, "I've got a young widow in the church whom I'd like to call. Her name is Betty Jo. Maybe she could give you a room for the night. A good meal and a clean bed will make all the difference in the world. Tomorrow we'll talk some more."

She seemed pleased. Someone cared. Someone was concerned. It would have been easier to put her in a hotel, but she might have had second thoughts about that bridge. The safest thing was to have her with someone who would look out for her.

Arrangements were soon completed and Betty Jo was on her way to pick Gloria up at the station. When Betty Jo arrived, I briefed her on Gloria's problems and then made a parting shot to Gloria herself:

"Try giving God a chance in your life. Start tonight. He's there to help when life looks bleak. Before you go to bed, pray. See what a difference it makes!"

She had a defeated expression on her face as she said, "I'll try again, Reverend, but you might as well know, I've *been* praying and nothing's happened so far."

Betty Jo phoned the next morning, giving me the name of Gloria's sweetheart and additional information about Gloria herself who arrived at my office before nine o'clock, looking like a new woman. Clean, her hair neatly combed, she was quite attractive in Betty Jo's dress. There was an alertness about her that was missing when I had last seen her.

Someone needed to get this girl's life straightened out. Her outlook and perspective had to change, and I knew that only God could accomplish it. He and He alone could supply the motivation she needed to become a changed person. And only His Holy Spirit could supply the Power.

"O Lord," I prayed silently, "help me give Gloria some new insights; cause her to let You into her life and her plans."

I knew that before the day was over several things had to be accomplished. I was going to have to tell Gloria that I knew her lover (a prominent attorney) and that I knew where he was now living. She needed to see the folly of chasing a man who didn't love her and accept the responsibility of returning to her four children who did love and need her.

"Gloria," I said, "Franklin left Fort Myers several months ago and began a new law practice in Jacksonville."

"You know him," she cried. "And you know where he is. I must go to him. He loves me—I know he does. I've got to go to Jacksonville and see him. I just must!"

"Gloria, it's a hopeless cause, and you'll die in the chase.

Maybe if the man ever gets his own personal life straightened out—but right now he's running away from you just as hard as you're running toward him."

She bit her lip, fighting to keep back the tears.

"I'm going to make a telephone call, Gloria," I said, "to locate your children. If your neighbor has had second thoughts about your leaving, your children may be in the hands of the juvenile authorities already. You'll be charged with desertion and declared an unfit mother. If the courts get into this picture by taking custody of your children, you'll have a pretty difficult time getting them back."

The reminder that she might lose her children threw a new light on the subject. She became cooperative, giving telephone numbers, names and addresses of people to call. I slid the phone across the desk and suggested she begin dialing.

As she lifted the receiver, I said, "Remember, Gloria, after you've found out about the children and have made certain that they're being well taken care of, you're going right back to Fort Walton Beach tonight."

"You mean I've got to leave today and go back?" she asked.

"Yes, ma'am, that's exactly what I mean. You'll be back there tonight. And you're going to get a job! I know you think it's beneath your dignity to work. But you've got some responsibilities that you can't avoid—four children to care for until they're old enough to care for themselves. Betty Jo told me earlier this morning that you're a top-notch legal secretary and these gals are always in demand. You'll get a job. And while all this is taking place you're going to develop your spiritual resources. You can't do this alone, I know. But you can do it through the strength and daily encouragement that God can give you. If you believe in Him, then you must believe that with Him all things are possible."

Gloria nodded and looked hopeful for the first time.

"I prayed last night at Betty Jo's house," she said. "I asked

God for strength and help with all these battles I'm fighting. Most of all I just asked for strength to get me safely through the night and back here."

"Do you go to church in Fort Walton Beach?" I asked.

"No, sir, we don't go to church anymore. I haven't been in years."

"All of us need God's help, Gloria. Life's problems have a way of being lifted when we share them with Him. Truly, He is our refuge and strength, our very present help in time of trouble." She nodded as if she was realizing some of these things already.

I began making arrangements for her trip back to Fort Walton Beach, checking schedules and transportation costs.

"Gloria, we'll pay your transportation costs, provide some money for meals, and give you some additional funds for groceries when you get home," I said. "I realize this isn't much—but it's a beginning. At least you won't be walking into that trailer tonight with an empty purse."

"I'll pay you back, honest I will," she promised, tucking the money I'd given her into the top of her dress. "Just as soon as I get a job and have some income. I'll pay back everything," she said tearfully.

"It isn't going to be necessary to pay us back, Gloria. We've been repaid if we've helped you straighten out your life," I said, really believing she might make it and wishing we could do more to help.

It was approaching noon, and her bus left at 1:30 P.M. I suggested she have lunch with my secretary and then we'd take her to the bus terminal for the trip home. Just before we left the office I turned and asked, "Gloria, would you let me pray for you and your children?"

"I'd appreciate it and want you to," she whispered.

After I had prayed God's blessing on her and her children, I said, "Amen."

"Oh, yes, God," she added. "And please help us to know You're real."

As she boarded the bus I gave her one of my calling cards.

"Gloria, when you get home tonight I want you to call me collect. I want to know that you made it back safely, and let you have the chance to discuss anything else that we might have forgotten about today."

I wasn't begging for collect telephone calls, but it was the safest way to handle it. The long-distance operator would give me the origin of the call, and I'd know if she had gone home or jumped the bus and headed elsewhere.

Gloria did call later that evening—from Fort Walton Beach. A week later I heard from her again. She had located a job with a law firm, and was pleased with her work.

A few weeks elapsed before she wrote again to tell me that she and the children were attending a small Methodist church where the children were enrolled in Sunday school.

I still hear from Gloria, and she shares her happiness and remembers with gratitude how her life was changed one night when she walked into a police station.

"Religion," she wrote in one of her letters, "is a real meaningful part of our lives."

VI. A BAD SCENE

Do you not know that your body is a temple of the Holy Spirit . . . ? (I Cor. 6:19).

There wasn't much conversation between the lieutenant and me as we drove through the quiet streets of the city to the hospital.

"Two teenagers freaked out on an overdose of something," the dispatcher had said.

Sometimes, when answering a call, I was just plain scared! Again, I often found myself thinking about the best way to handle the problem tactfully. I wasn't really scared this time; I was doing a little thinking, and a lot of praying!

"God," I caught myself saying, "how come? How come we've got a drug problem in our community? Five years ago a narcotics arrest was unheard of in Fort Myers. Now we've got a problem reaching epidemic proportions. Why, Lord, do they do it? Whose fault is it that these kids are being turned on by drugs? We've got more churches here than we've ever had, and still we're failing. If we've got two kids at the hospital now, there must be several dozen others scattered throughout the city that we don't even know about. Lord, please, please help us to find the answers."

"Check us out, Rev," the lieutenant said, interrupting my thought process.

I looked up, found we had arrived at the emergency room of the hospital, and picked up the mike to call the station. *Well,* I was thinking, *let's get in there and see what we've got. Let's see if it really is a bad scene.*

It was!

The waiting room was crammed with weirdly dressed teenagers who cast hateful glances at us as we walked through the doors. They didn't say it, but we knew what they were thinking. We were the "PIGS" probably about to "bust" a couple of their friends. One long-haired, bearded kid approached us and ordered us to let the boys go.

"It's their life," he said. "Let them do what they want with it. They aren't hurting anyone. Your copper friends snatched them up and hauled them off to this place. You guys never would have caught them if they'd had a few more minutes to get ready for their trip. You came along too soon."

"Cool it, man," I said sternly. "No one said your friends were going to be arrested. We're trying to help. What did they take? That medical staff in the back can't do much until they know what to give these boys to counteract the drugs. It would help—" I was interrupted abruptly and rudely:

"It's none of your damn business what they took. Just let them go," the boy commanded.

The lieutenant doesn't put up with much of that lip for long:

"Young man, either you sit down and shut up until we find out what this is all about," he pointed to a chair, "or you'll be booked on a disorderly conduct charge!" His tone of voice made it clear that he meant business.

The young man sat down.

Moving into the treatment area of the emergency room, we found the two boys. The younger of the two was tripping the light fantastic up and down the corridor, completely oblivious of anything going on around him. For the time being he wasn't going to bother anyone.

The second boy was a different story. A couple of officers, two nurses, an aide, and the resident physician were standing around him. None were very sympathetic with his condition. The officers had not yet removed his handcuffs, since he was hallucinating badly, acting violent, and shouting four-letter words.

The resident physician, slowly losing his patience, asked if I could find out from some of his "hippie" friends what he had taken.

"Better find out something, Rev," he said; "I'm not going to listen to this foulmouthed kid all night long."

"Look, Doc," I said, "right now he needs help before he hurts himself or someone else, and like it or not we've got a responsibility to try to bring him down as humanely as we possibly can." With that I headed back to the waiting room.

I spotted a couple of kids I knew and called them into the consultation room.

"I'll put it to you honestly," I said. "One of your friends back there is in bad shape. He's on a bad trip. No one has been busted, and I don't think anyone will be—but we've got to know what he had or what he's taken and how long ago it was. If you care about your friend at all, you'll tell me."

"Mr. Asmuth," one of the girls said, "I don't want to rat on anyone, much less a friend. He hasn't caused any trouble. Just let him go. We'll take care of him."

I could feel my fuse getting shorter and thought, *Lord, don't let me lose my cool or we'll never get anywhere with these kids. I need to rap with them more than I've ever needed to before.*

"Listen, gals," I said. "That Book I preach from and believe in tells us that we ARE our brother's keeper. If you want to help him, and help him right now, then tell me what it was. I don't care where he got it. I just want to know what it was."

"Promise?" one of them said. "Promise that they won't bust the boys or us?"

"I promise. You can depend on that," I told them, hoping they'd believe me.

"They both dropped some acid," one said. "Tell us, will they be all right?"

"I hope so," I said and returned to the treatment area.

"Doc," I said, "both boys dropped acid. Can you do something to bring them out of it?"

He nodded, taking one of the nurses with him to prepare an injection for the boy. *Maybe, just maybe,* I thought, *we can begin to talk him down. It's worth a try if we can get some of the people out of the room.* I suggested that it would be best if a few were to leave. They got the message, and all but two of them left the room.

The lad was now sitting calmly in a chair with the cuffs on. He complained that the cuffs were hurting his wrists. He wanted them off. Speaking gently we told him if he would get up on the examining table and lie down we would remove the cuffs. His mood changing from one of utter confusion to an awareness of his present surroundings, he cooperated and did as we asked. We tried talking with him to relieve his fears and it looked as if we were progressing nicely. But our progress was short-lived. The drug in the bloodstream flared up again and suddenly he was maniacal—worse than before. He sensed that he could fly and tried to do so, landing with an abrupt thud on the hard floor. Others heard the commotion and came rushing in. He kicked, bit, snarled, and fought. He hadn't really come down at all—he was still tripping, and tripping badly!

The doctor was back with the injection, but nothing could be done until the boy was subdued. It meant the cuffs again, and probably restraining straps once he was back on the examining table. In time I'll forget what I heard him say, but I'll never forget how he acted. It was a scene I wished his parents could have seen, a scene I would like to have shared with all his admirers and friends in the waiting room. It might have straightened some of them out—for good.

Eventually the boy was back on the examining table, secured with restraining straps, but still trying to thresh about. The shot was given and ever so slowly the evil spirits were subdued, and he drifted off into a deep sleep.

In the morning it would all be like a bad dream. He was going to ache from his excessive struggling and threshing. He was also going to have some bruises to show as a result of his flight from the table to the floor, as well as some marks on his wrists where he tried to work off the handcuffs. These were all minor, though, compared to the impending threat of nightmarish flashbacks over a prolonged period of time. When, how many, how severe, how long would they last? Who can tell? There just aren't any answers that can be given.

The parents? Where were they? Had anyone tried to reach them? What would they say and think when they arrived? The hospital staff advised us that they had been trying—unsuccessfully—to reach the parents.

"Advise us when you reach them," said the lieutenant. "We'd like to talk with them before they take the boy home."

I knew what he was thinking. We had to talk with the parents before that boy was released. He'd have to be watched throughout the night, and they needed an explanation of just what the circumstances were. His dirty and bruised body could cause them to think of police brutality unless they realized the youth had inflicted these things upon himself.

The waiting-room hecklers had grown tired and left, leaving behind the second boy who was still gaily and happily wandering through the halls. He offered no resistance at all when I suggested we sit down and have a talk. Everything was beautiful—even me—as we chatted together in the conference room. He just unloaded and emptied everything that was on his heart and soul.

His name was Alex. Both his parents were dead, and he was living with legal guardians appointed by the court. He was fifteen, had failed a couple of grades in school, but had never been in any real trouble with the authorities. He didn't go to church, and was not too knowledgeable as to what churches were for or what happened when you went to one.

"What about tonight, Alex?" I asked. "Do you want to tell me where you got the stuff, and how you got the bread?"

"Oh, sure, man! It was real easy, but first I thought I'd been taken. I was at The Inn and this guy was going around the room trying to get people to buy little white pills. Everybody was popping them. Well, this guy came up to me and said, 'Hey man, how about you? You want one of these pills? It'll make you feel good, real good, man.' "

"So you put down the bread and bought the pill?"

"Sort of," he said. "I'm a busboy at that big restaurant downtown—you know the one. The tips had been good, and I had lots of bread, lots of bread, man. The pills were so tiny, I thought I'd buy two. I gave the man ten dollars, and he gave me two pills."

"Did you drop both of them?"

"No, I was going to, but everyone said I'd better be careful. I ate about half of the first one, waited awhile, and nothing happened. Would you believe? Absolutely nothing happened." His voice squeaked off into a high falsetto. "I figured I'd been gypped, or the pill hadn't had time to work. *Why not take the rest of the pill?* I said to myself, and popped it in. Then it happened. It was beautiful."

"Can you remember what happened, Alex? Can you describe your feelings and what you saw?" I asked.

"I was in heaven, and I was the king," Alex related. "You could see music everywhere. The room was full of music everywhere you looked. And pictures! You could hear them talking to you. Everything was beautiful. It was like being in a new kind of world. It was wonderful—but there's one thing that's bothering me." He squirmed in his clothes and tried to look over his shoulder.

"What's that, Alex?" I didn't understand.

"This monkey that's on my back. See him there? I can feel him crawling around on my back. I reach and swat, but can't seem to reach him or catch him. He's always getting away."

Still hallucinating, I shuddered. Alex was coming down off his trip, but the chemical monster was still working away in his bloodstream.

"Reverend," Alex said, interrupting my thought process, "I itch and burn all over. There must have been something in that police car that brought me here to the hospital. I just can't stop itching. My arms, my stomach—it's real bad. And, I almost feel as if I'm on fire and going to burn up any moment. Please make it stop. It's just got to stop! I can't stand it any longer!" He was screaming by then.

Why had the boy done this to himself? He wasn't all to blame. Peer-group pressure had a lot to do with it. His environment—the insecurity of the home where he was living—didn't help either. The cards were not exactly stacked in his favor. Yet he was a child of the Creator with a potential that was undeveloped. He could go in either direction—which one would be determined by whose influence was the strongest—the secular world's or that of the Christian church.

God, I was praying, *help us save this boy from a life of disaster. I know he is precious in Your sight.*

The door of the consultation room opened. It was the lieutenant telling me that Alex's guardians were there to take the boy home.

"Loot," I asked, "may I speak with them and the boy before they leave?"

Our conversation was brief and to the point. I asked Alex and his guardians if they would come to my office on Monday morning, indicating that Alex should be watched carefully since he could be subject to flashbacks at any time.

"Are there any charges against Alex?" the woman asked.

"No, ma'am, there are no charges against either boy," the lieutenant answered. "We'd like to see that they get the help they need to straighten out their lives. We are, however, looking for the ones who are responsible for selling and pushing the drug upon these kids."

They thanked us as they left and promised to bring Alex in to see me Monday. I hoped the promise would be fulfilled.

"Lieutenant, what about the other boy's parents? Have they reached them yet?" I asked.

"Still no answer," he said, "but they'll keep trying. The lad is sound asleep—looks quite angelic lying on the examining table."

"He may *look* angelic," I said. "But this drug scene is sure turning into a devilish problem."

He agreed with me, shaking his head in despair.

"You know, Loot," I went on, "we've had two kids die this year from an overdose of drugs. We've had almost 150 arrests so far, and the year isn't over!

"I've been working with a little gal in her late teens who is trying to kick her habit. You know what started it? NO ONE CARED! She started moving with the wrong crowd; then came the pot parties with the grass. It wasn't strong enough.

One night she dropped some acid and had a bad trip. It was after the bad trip that she wandered in. She wanted to kick it, but needed help. It was six months ago when she dropped acid and she's still flashing. And each time she flashes it's a bad trip.

"Her circle of friends is smaller now, but they're better people. She runs scared everytime she has a flashback, gasps for breath and feels that she is going to die. It's a struggle for life when this happens. She wants to know how much longer it will last, and where it will end. It's rough keeping her buoyed up when you know these trips could continue for another year or a year and a half. However, her changed attitude is already an inspiration and a challenge to other young people who want to kick the habit."

The lieutenant had been listening thoughtfully. "How do you know, Rev, that she won't take it up again?" he asked.

"I don't know, Loot. I do know that God believes in her and loves her in spite of her failures and shortcomings. If He believes in her, I can too. And I plan to help see her through."

"I guess what bothers me, Rev, is that your kid or mine could get hooked on the stuff as easy as anyone's," the lieutenant said with grave concern.

"You're right," I said. "That's why it's important that we give them the moral and spiritual values they need to make sound judgments and decisions when put to the test. If they're spiritually strong they don't need drugs to turn them on. They'll make it. But, it's up to you, me, and the church to impart these values," I preached.

"How many kids have you talked with about drugs and narcotics, Rev?" asked the lieutenant.

"Too many to really remember. And with mixed results," I added. "It's not only kids, though; I get lots of parents. Some by themselves and some with their kids. I've talked to several thousand through our drug presentations in the school system. Perhaps it's from these programs that I get the kids and their parents. Some come to tease, test, and challenge. Others come because they've got a problem, need help, and know they can't lick it on their own. The parents, well, they either suspect their child is on drugs or have firsthand knowledge of it. The parents in most cases have had a complete breakdown in communication between their teenaged son or daughter.

"I don't want to see any kid get in trouble with the law," I explained. "The present laws make drug possession a felony, and you know what that means to their careers if they're convicted. They've blown everything and have pretty bad odds of ever becoming much of anything. It means we've got to get to them and get through to them before they become addicts or are busted. You can't force yourself upon them, but simply be available and let them know that you are there when they are ready to come. You can't use scare tactics either. You tell it like it is, giving them the facts and the risk factors. The decision is then in their hands. Once the decision to kick is made, they'll crawl on broken glass to get the help they need. The help can be medical, psychological, spiritual, legal, or a combination of all. But, they'll come when they need you and feel they can trust you."

I saw the lieutenant looking at his watch, and I realized that we had to get back in service, but I couldn't resist one more statement. "We did the right thing with these boys, Lieutenant."

"What do you mean the 'right thing,' Rev?" he wanted to know.

"We didn't arrest them and lock them up in jail. I knew it had to be your decision and I'm pleased with how you handled it. Putting them in jail for the night really wouldn't have solved a thing. The problem would still be there in the morning and in a sense it will be anyway. But at least we've got half a chance to establish some rapport with the boys, maybe rap with them a little bit, and get at the crux of their problems. I hope we've won a couple of friends who understand that we do other things besides crack skulls and put people behind bars!"

"Maybe you're right," he said, motioning me toward the door.

We made one more check with the staff, asking if they had reached the other boy's parents. Still no luck.

"We'll keep checking with you. We'd like to talk with them before the boy is discharged," the lieutenant said as we left the building and walked to the car.

The station dispatcher didn't have anything for us when we checked in, so the pressure was off for a short time. We chatted more about the drug and narcotic traffic in the county and remembered well the mass confusion we had with five teenagers several years ago when we were first introduced to the drug culture.

The five youngsters, in a car, were acting in a suspicious manner. They were stopped by one of the patrolmen. He assumed they were all intoxicated and brought them down to the station. But once in the booking room the patrolmen were confused. Not one of the five had any of the symptoms normally associated with alcohol. Rather, they all were extremely talkative with high-pitched voices—even the boys! They were drooling at the mouth, had widely dilated pupils in their eyes, and a little slur in their speech. There was no hint of alcohol on their breath. It was confusing to say the least.

The lieutenant and I were called in. We were equally confused, except for the detection of an unfamiliar odor about them. The odor in the car was even stronger. We had our suspicions, but upon a search of the vehicle could find nothing.

A car was dispatched to the area where the five had been apprehended and a search begun for some evidence. The officers discovered a pint-sized can of cleaning fluid that had been almost emptied, and several rags that had been saturated with the liquid.

The pieces were now falling together—these kids were high on cleaning fluid. It was a new experience for us, and we were not fully aware of the inherent dangers. The kids were all a happy bunch, registering their bewilderment as to why they had been brought to the police station and wanting to know what the charges were. We didn't have any now. The officers at the scene thought they did, but the only thing to do was to call the parents, advise them of the infraction, and let the kids go home.

That night, we recalled, served as our introduction to the whole new world of drugs and narcotics. Now, it's a different story and picture. Today if a kid has ten dollars and ten minutes he can get anything he wants if he has the right contacts. It's here, and in spite of the arrests, convictions, and crackdowns, the "cow" is continuing to grow fat, and we find it almost impossible to kill.

We continued to talk as the lieutenant headed the car in the direction of the high river bridge.

"Where are you going, Loot?" I asked.

"Just thought I'd take this car out on the highway, open 'er up for a change, blow some of the carbon out!" he replied. "This city driving gums things up, so we'll give her a good run for a few minutes."

The city lighting system ends on the north end of the bridge, but the city line is several hundred yards further to the north. We were slowing down to turn around at the city line when my eyes detected a figure standing at the side of the road in the darkness.

"Loot, Loot," I exclaimed. "Over there. A little boy standing beside the road. Let's have a look."

The little fellow had blond hair, blue eyes, and was about

four feet high. He was standing there in white T-shirt, blue jeans, bare feet, and with his thumb in the air. He couldn't have been more than six or seven years old. He was hitchhiking north.

Our unmarked car saved the day. If the little fellow had seen the markings and red lights on a police cruiser, I'm certain he would have run. We stopped and before he realized who we were, he asked if we'd take him for a ride. Then, seeing the uniforms, he burst into tears.

VII. WHY RUN?

Even a child makes himself known by his acts . . .
(Prov. 20:11).

If you were six years old, had run away from home, and faced a dark terrifying unknown vastness ahead of you, you'd cry too. The little tyke was crying so badly he was on the verge of hysterics. He wanted to run away. He knew where he was going. Yet he knew it was wrong. Now he had been caught.

I placed a fatherly arm about the little fellow, stooping to his height and trying to assure him everything was going to be all right. I wiped away the tears saying, "Little friend, you don't have to be afraid anymore. We're your friends and we're going to help you."

The faintest smile broke on his face, and I knew he was going to trust us. I slipped him into the front seat between us, and we began to chat.

"Son," I said, "what's your name, and where do you live?"

"Tommy, sir, Tommy Stewart," he said. "I live at 4747 Tiger Tail Avenue. I'm six years old and in the first grade at Cabbage Key School." His eyes began to well up as he fought the tears. "But I don't want to go home," he said. "If you take me back I'll just run away again. Don't take me home—please don't."

The lieutenant called the dispatcher and asked if they had a signal 10 (missing person) on a white male, Tommy Stewart, age six. Tommy was fascinated by the two-way radio. Within seconds the dispatcher gave us a negative answer. This meant his folks either hadn't reported it, or Tommy had slipped out of the house while the family was asleep.

"Tommy," I asked, "don't you think your mommy and daddy will wonder where you are and be worried about you?"

"They don't love me. They told me if I didn't like my home I could just get out and go live somewhere else. That's why I left. I'm going to see my grandmother in Alabama," he sniffed.

"Tommy, it's a long way to Alabama," I said, handing him my handkerchief.

"I know it," he replied, blowing his nose noisily. "But I can get there. I've got a road map in my pocket. My gramma lives in Montgomery. I'm going to live with her." He was a determined little fellow, not easily discouraged.

"You need money when you travel, Tommy," I reminded him.

"Yes, sir, 'n' I got money with me," he said, reaching in his pocket. "Don't you think this is enough?" He pulled out eight pennies.

"Those eight pennies won't take you very far, Tommy," I said, trying to keep from laughing out loud—or crying with him. "Besides, you're barefoot, and it gets a lot colder at night when you get up north." I was hoping to discourage him, but he was way ahead of me. He reached into another pocket and brought out a pair of clean white socks.

"I can put these on my feet when the ground gets too cold—they'll keep me warm," he said confidently. His well-thought-out plot was very touching and made me want to take him home with me.

"Tommy, we're going to go down to the police station so we can talk some more," I said. "Maybe we can help."

It didn't take Tommy long to capture the hearts of the boys at the station. One of the officers knew the Stewarts.

"They're a couple of barflies," he explained. "Chances are they aren't home yet. I'll bet the boy was told to sit in the car while they were in the tavern getting stoned. I don't blame the kid for running away. I'd run, too, if I had that kind of a home life."

If they are drunk, I thought, *I'd rather not deal with them tonight. Besides, they'd probably knock the stuffing out of the kid for taking off.*

"Please," Tommy said, interrupting my thoughts, "let me stay here. I won't cause you no trouble. I'll be good, I promise I will."

"But, Tommy," said one of the uniformed men, "we don't have anyplace to keep you. This is a police station and out back is the jail with hard beds, cold cells, and lots of real bad guys."

"Oh, that's all right. It's better than home. Here you laugh and joke and have fun. All my parents do is fight, drink, and beat me up."

One of the officers called me aside: "Rev, little Tommy is right. That poor kid doesn't have any home life at all. His parents hardly know what it is to draw a sober breath. Maybe we can all help; at least I'm willing to do what I can for the boy's sake."

These guys have soft hearts, I thought. *They've got love and compassion when the chips are down.* I remembered the words of Isaiah, "and a little child shall lead them." Little Tommy was leading all of us tonight. I walked into the radio room.

"Mr. Gorrell," I said to the dispatcher, "could you send a car to the Stewarts' residence on Tiger Tail Avenue? Let's see if Tommy's parents are home. We've got to begin somewhere."

"Will do, Rev," he answered, calling for the zone five car and giving a condensed version of the problem.

I looked around for Tommy and found he had corralled one of the uniformed men. The two were walking hand in hand down the corridor, jabbering away, with Tommy firing a barrage of questions at the officer. He was fascinated by his surroundings, experiencing one of the rare moments in his life when he felt loved and wanted.

Well-adjusted, happy children don't run away from home, I thought. *When they receive love, affection, and sound spiritual values they seldom think of leaving. Yet, how many of these runaways have been victims of BAD PARENTS?*

I remembered the twelve-year-old boy we found about three o'clock one morning hitchhiking on the main highway. He said his father had kicked him out and told him he never wanted to see him again. We verified his story, and reluctantly turned him over to the juvenile authorities in his home county about two hundred miles to the north of us. I never heard any more about him, but just prayed the juvenile courts could place the lad in a foster home where he WOULD be wanted and loved.

Then there was Linda, barely fourteen years old when we found her shivering, huddled behind a rock formation on the east coast late one night. She hadn't come home from school that afternoon and her parents had come to the station to report her missing.

"She's a bad girl," her father said, "but we'll get her

straightened out when you folks find her." While her stepmother shed buckets of crocodile tears, I picked her father's brain. They were trying to put up a good front for the sake of the authorities, but they really didn't want her back at all.

"Mr. Jones," I asked, "if we do find your daughter do we have your permission to take her to the juvenile authorities? Perhaps they are the best ones to determine what disciplinary measures should be taken to prevent this again."

They gave their approval. Linda, I discovered, had run away several times before and also had a record with juvenile authorities in several different states. Maybe she was "a bad girl" as her daddy had implied, but maybe she wasn't ALL bad. Maybe with the right approach she could be redeemed and salvaged. The immediate problem, though, was to find her.

A missing person's bulletin was issued in a four-county area. Luckily we found her. I expected her to run from us, too. But she was cold and frightened by the pounding of the surf in the black of the night, and was actually relieved at being caught.

"But if you take me home to my father, I'll run again before you get to the front door," she threatened. "He reported me missing because he just wanted to make it look like he cared. He hates me—I know he does. That slut he married has convinced him I'm no good. She even told him I should be put in the detention home. Take me there if you want, but don't take me home." Linda was confused and frightened, but I believed her firm words about not wanting to go home.

"I'm not making any promises about what will happen," I said. "We'll do one thing at a time. Right now we're taking you down to the station where we can sit and talk through your problem. Then we'll try to make some decisions."

In her thirteen years Linda had never lived anywhere with anyone longer than six months at a time. She had been conceived and born out of wedlock, and she had no idea where her mother was now living, or with whom. She had lived with her in Wisconsin; consequently, she was placed in a foster home in that state. She was also on probation.

"Why probation, Linda?" I asked.

"I was caught fighting again on the schoolgrounds with another girl after I'd been warned before."

"Was this in Wisconsin?" I asked.

"Yes, sir, it was."

"How is it that you are now living with your father?"

"Well, my father had just married this woman when all this happened. They were going to move to Florida. I didn't like these people I was living with anyway, and I knew they would put me in detention after the fight. My father found out and had a talk with the judge. I was released in his custody."

"Have you been in any trouble with the Florida authorities?"

"No, not until today. You see, we've only been here two weeks. I don't like it down here; I want to go back to Wisconsin."

"You'd go back to Wisconsin, knowing that you'd be placed in juvenile detention?"

"I'd rather go back there and be placed in detention than have to live with my old man and that woman he married." Her face was so in earnest that I sympathized with her completely and conferred with the lieutenant privately.

"Loot, I know what the law says we should do, but let's *bend* the law just a little if we can." I tried to keep the pleading out of my voice.

"What've you got in mind, Rev?" he asked.

"Just notify Linda's parents and tell them you have her in protective custody. That's all."

"What do you propose to do with the girl?" he asked, looking through me in that way he had.

"I'll let you know just as soon as I call my wife, Violet," I confessed sheepishly.

"Rev, you're getting softhearted again," he teased. "You know she'll run just as soon as she has the chance. You've had it happen before, you know."

"I know, Loot, but I'm willing to take the chance, and give her one at the same time. I don't think she'll run before the hearing with the juvenile authorities, though."

A phone call was all it took. I knew Linda would have a clean bed and good meal waiting when we arrived at the house.

We didn't wait long for the court hearing. Linda, her father and stepmother, and Violet and I all attended. The attitude of Linda's folks was pretty evident to the judge. He quickly sensed that they did not want the girl living with them.

"Reverend Asmuth," he asked, "would you and your wife be willing to take custody of the child for six months?" Before we had a chance to answer, he added, "We'll set up another hearing at that time and be governed accordingly."

We gave our approval and he conferred with each of us privately. He placed Linda on probation and introduced her to her juvenile counselor to whom she would report weekly.

There were problems with Linda, but over the weeks we could begin to see gradual improvement. Her attitudes were changing. She became willing to assume responsibilities around the house. And she enjoyed our children as much as they enjoyed her. For the first time in her life she was introduced to church. It was a foreign experience, and she had some difficulty grasping the meaning of it all at first. But that came also, with time.

She participated regularly in the youth program, attended Sunday school, and worshiped with the family on Sundays. We had talks with her about Christ and the difference He could make in her life. All she had to do was accept Him, and confess Him as Lord and Savior. It was going to come, but she wasn't quite ready to take the step. There was a marked improvement in her school grades, and we were encouraged with her progress. It was almost too good to be true.

Then it happened.

Two days before Christmas there was a telephone call from her father. I still don't know what the conversation was all about, but that night Linda was gone. We'd taken her to a dance and told her we'd pick her up at 11:00 P.M. I was early, but the other kids said she had left shortly after she arrived. She and a boy had gone off in a car. I knew who the boy was, and it was bad news! It meant trouble. Her father had no doubt said something over the phone to upset Linda. I was sure this was why she had run.

I searched the county all night long. Even though it was Saturday night and tomorrow was Christmas Eve (with four services scheduled at the church) I was determined to find her. At four o'clock in the morning we found the boy and the car, but no Linda. He refused to talk, and I was tired and upset, and my temper had a short fuse. I took him to the station so he could sit and think it over. Slowly it came out, every ugly detail. The boy seemed completely honest.

"Her father called today," he began, "and said he was going to the judge and make her come home. She wanted me to take her away, take her anyplace. But I wasn't going to get into that kind of trouble. I just took her out, got her good and drunk, and introduced her to sex. I never intended to help her. I was just after her body." He shrugged his shoulders matter-of-factly, as if he had no realization he had done wrong.

I wanted to shake him. It was a critical moment. It took every ounce of my energy to keep my internal rage from becoming external. But neither the lieutenant nor I reacted openly. We just waited.

"Where is she now?" the lieutenant asked coldly.

"She's in the front seat of the Reverend's other car at his house, passed out like a light. I carried her to his car and just dumped her on the front seat," he said. Utterly dejected, I left the station and found Linda where he said she was—in a drunken stupor. I couldn't waken her and just carried her to her bed. I gave an abbreviated version of the story to Violet and tried to catch some shut-eye before leaving for the four services ahead of me.

Linda later related the facts corroborating the boy's story. She had been terrified by her father's phone call, hit the panic button, and was embarrassed by the series of events that had followed.

A doctor's examination revealed that she was not pregnant. We tried to reassure her that she was with us by court order and that she could be removed only by an action of the court. Still the fear persisted. The chain of events opened the door for a candid talk between her and my wife about sex. That single sexual experience could result in her being badly maladjusted for the rest of her life. We didn't want to see this happen. We knew, too, that she had great potential, and we wanted to help her develop her good points.

Several months passed before another mysterious call from her father. Another trauma followed. We watched her closely, fearing the call would trigger some unexpected reaction. But when? A call from the school officials one morning brought the answer.

"Was Linda sick this morning?" the secretary asked.

"No, I drove her to school myself," I answered.

"She never made it to homeroom, and neither did the girl she runs around with," the woman informed me.

I thanked her and started thinking. *If she's with Bess, then chances are good the boy that got Linda drunk at Christmastime is with them too.* It had been rumored he and Bess were going to run away to Georgia and get married.

I made a few phone calls. Bess's parents were upset because Bess was gone. The boy hadn't shown up on his job. It was evident that the three of them were together. We put out a missing-person's bulletin on the two girls and a pick-up-and-hold on the boy.

Two uneventful days passed. At midnight on the second day a teletype came through from the sheriff's department in an upper Florida east-coast county. They had picked up the three runaways and were holding them. By return teletype we advised them we were on our way. On the long drive north the lieutenant asked what I was going to do with the girls when I brought them back.

"Sir, they're both going directly to the juvenile home. I try to keep my promises. I told Linda at Christmas that if she ever took off again she'd go directly to the juvenile detention home and her fate would then be decided by the judge. She's got to learn that she can't keep running forever. It's too bad, because she was doing beautifully, but now she's blown it all." It hurt me that we had failed with her.

"Maybe you should ask the judge for a restraining order against the father which would forbid his even calling the house," the lieutenant suggested. I could follow through on that after we found her, if—

Some three hours later we found ourselves in an east coast county jail talking to all three kids. Linda had been dumped by Bess and her boyfriend, and had been picked up first by the deputies. The other two were picked up moments later. Bess and the boy had planned on driving to Georgia to be married.

The boy was mean and cagey, so the lieutenant borrowed a pair of handcuffs and fastened his hands together under his legs. It was awkward, but he wasn't going to get away this time. The lieutenant drove the boy's car with the boy in it, while I took the girls in the other, placing them in the back seat.

The long trip back was made in complete silence, broken only once when I informed the girls that our destination was the juvenile detention home. Reluctantly they came out of the car to be greeted by the matron. There were no good-byes, just sobs, as they made their way to their temporary new home.

The judge, juvenile counselor, and I all agreed that a two-week stay in detention would be good therapy, followed by a court hearing and whatever action was necessary. Both girls were given stiff probations and forbidden to see each other.

It changed Linda. She became more serious about her religion now. She was studying the Bible, asking questions, and preparing to unite with the Church at Easter. On Easter day, along with several other young people, she made her confession of faith in Jesus Christ. She was sensing that answers could be found in the light of her religious convictions and faith. She was learning, too, that prayer does change things.

Her father still called, but he no longer had a frightening effect upon her. She seemed to be able to relate to him. The school year finished, and her grades were good. Her attitude in the home was improving. We could trust her and knew that God was guiding and helping her. Her probationary period ended and she was given her freedom. How pleased with the progress and results we were! It had taken almost a year, but Linda was a changed person. Could it last, and for how long?

I received a call from her father early in the summer. He and his wife wanted to come and have a talk with me. They wanted to talk about Linda.

The appointed hour for their visit arrived and I was tense. I had a premonition that they wanted Linda back to live with them. I was right!

Linda's father was being transferred by his employer to the Carolinas and they wanted Linda to go north with them.

"Mr. Asmuth," he said, "we'd like to have Linda come and live with us. I love her and know you folks have taken good care of her, but I'd like to have her back with us. Do you think she will come?"

"I don't know," I replied. "Linda's come a long way in the year that we've had her. It's as if a miracle had taken place, but I just don't know. I'll talk to Violet and to Linda and let you know."

Violet and I talked and prayed about Linda's future and what we should say and how to say it. It seemed best, in the final analysis, for Linda to join her father and stepmother.

"Linda," we said to her one evening after the other children had been bedded down for the night, "your father called the other day. He's being transferred to the Carolinas, and he wants you to join him and the family. They want you to go with them. You don't have to go. You're welcome to stay here with us if this is your desire." I watched closely for her reaction. "I'm sure that the judge will be fair and open-minded about the matter. This is perhaps one of the biggest decisions you've ever had to make. We love you and will keep you, but you've got to decide," I sympathized. "I know, too, that your father loves you. Maybe our prayers for him have been answered, because he's very sincere in wanting you back.

"One of three things is going to happen now Linda, and you've got to pray about all three. You can stay with us, you can go back with your father, or you can run. However, if you run this time you're going to be running the rest of your life. Mrs. Asmuth and I can't decide for you—it's got to be your decision. We don't want your answer tonight. We want you to pray about it, and we'll pray about it. Then we'll talk again in the morning."

At the breakfast table we waited for Linda to take the initiative. Her voice broke, tears started to come, and along with it her decision. She wanted to stay, but she knew her rightful place was with her dad.

"I'll call Daddy this morning," she said, "and tell him that I'll go north with them when they leave. But I'm going to miss you all so much, especially the children. They've become like my own, and I love them as much as I do you."

We knew she didn't want to leave, but she was facing her responsibilities and was now geared to cope with life.

"This isn't going to be easy, Linda," Violet said. "You're going to have to make adjustments, but you've learned here that family life involves giving and taking. And God will see you through. Your father's pleased that you're going to church, and he has promised to make this a family affair now. I'm sure that it will make a difference in your lives—life will be better for all of you because of God."

The juvenile judge was a personal friend whom I respected. On the day of the hearing when Linda was awarded to her father, he spoke with kindness and assurance. We knew Linda would make it.

"Before you leave, Linda," I said, "let me ask that you keep in touch with us. Write often and share some of the things that are on your mind. And, if your little world ever looks too glum or bleak, pick up that phone and call before you do something you might regret later on. I'm sure, whatever the problem, there will always be someone to help you see it through."

Linda wrote often. There were problems, but she stuck with it. She's now a young lady, and when we last heard from her, was still doing admirably. We often think about how God does make a difference in our lives and how He changed Linda's.

My reverie about our runaways was interrupted by one of the officers standing in the door:

"Hey, Rev," he said. "I want you to see something."

I followed him down the corridor and found little Tommy curled up sound asleep, clutching a half-eaten candy bar one of the men had bought him.

"You won't have to worry about him going to Alabama tonight," the officer said. "He's in dreamland for a little while and at peace with his world."

"What about his parents?" I asked.

"Oh, I guess Mr. Gorrell didn't tell you. They're both passed out in the car by the Polo Bar. The officer on the road couldn't awaken them. We'll just let them sleep it off, keeping a watch on the car throughout the night. Everyone may be in a better frame of mind after they've had a little sleep. After all, you'd rather talk with them when they're sober than when they're drunk, wouldn't you?"

"You're so right. My batting average with drunks is pretty bad," I said.

If I can find my lieutenant, I thought, *we can get our car back out on the road and see what the rest of the world is up to. I need some fresh air to wake me up or I'll be in the same predicament Tommy is in back there.* I was still hunting the lieutenant when Mr. Gorrell called to me:

"Rev," I heard him say, "we've got an unwed mother for you!"

"You've got to be kidding, Mr. Gorrell," I moaned. "I don't need any unwed mothers tonight along with everything else I've had," I pleaded.

Mr. Gorrell was like that, always coming up with little jokes to get a rise out of you in tense moments.

"Just kidding," he said, "but what did you do with the last one we gave you?"

Unwed mothers! I was saying to myself. *What* do *you do with 'em?*

VIII. I DON'T WANT IT!

Let him who is without sin among you be the first to throw a stone at her (John 8:7).

"That Debbie sure was a sight the night she walked into the station," dispatcher Allen Gorrell was saying. "I thought for a minute she was going to have that baby right here in the lobby."

"It was a rough case, all right, but all unwed mothers are difficult to handle, Allen," I told him. He nodded.

"These cases always seem harder, Rev. I wonder why—"

I thought about it for a minute.

Unwed mothers—or mothers-to-be—tormented with guilt feelings, realizing the wrongness of what they've done, are caught in a struggle to make a decision about the fate of the baby: *Shall I keep it? Shall I place it for adoption? Shall I have an abortion?*

Often the girl can point to a particular man and place the blame on him. Others, though, with looser morals, find that the father could be any one of several men.

There was the frantic plight of Debbie. Allen Gorrell called me about her late one night—

I'm an exceptionally sound sleeper. A Boeing 747 could rattle and shatter the bedroom windows and I'd never hear it.

But let that telephone ring and it's a changed scene! I'm clutching the cradle in my hand before it rings twice, and amaze myself at being alert and able to talk intelligently at three or four o'clock in the morning. Whenever the phone rings at that hour of the night (or morning) I know it's some kind of trouble, and I'd better be prepared to listen carefully and closely. Desperate folks give the message only once.

The night Allen Gorrell called me about Debbie, I was wide awake when I picked up the receiver.

"Rev," he sounded mildly apologetic, "this is Gorrell at the police station. Sorry about the hour, but we've got a huge unwed expectant mother who just walked in, and we'd like to have you come down and talk to her."

"Now?" I asked. "At whatever time it is?" It didn't *sound* like a right-now emergency to me. "Couldn't it wait till morning?"

"Nope, Rev," he answered. "Right now. She looks like she's about to have the baby right here in the lobby."

I got into my clothes and made it to the station in record time.

Debbie was not particularly attractive. Allen's descriptive phrase of "huge" was accurate. She was in her early twenties, had a natural weight problem without the pregnancy, and apparently had cried a lot before coming to the station. Her eyes were swollen and red. But she was semicomposed when I approached her and seemed relieved to find someone who would hear her out and perhaps offer to help.

Debbie was a willing talker who pulled no punches. She began at once to unload what was on her heart as if there was no time to waste. She had been a waitress at a local twenty-four-hour truck stop. She was single and had no living relatives. A high-school dropout in the tenth grade, she found job opportunities limited and was doing about the best she could.

The tips were good and while she had been working there were no financial problems.

She became friendly with one of the delivery-truck drivers. "It was nice," she said, "to have someone to talk with from time to time." The friendship between Debbie and the delivery man developed into a dating relationship, and later into a bedroom relationship. Soon he had moved into her apartment. He wanted to wait on marriage, he said. Debbie was in no hurry until she began to suspect she was pregnant.

A doctor verified her suspicions. It was then that her man told her the truth. They couldn't get married because he was already married. He and his wife were separated by agreement, yet he was continuing to see her from time to time, while he also carried on his steady affair with Debbie. She believed him when he promised her he would start divorce proceedings immediately so they could get married.

After several months, it became obvious to Debbie's friends and her employer that she had conceived a child out of wedlock. Her boyfriend kept making promises and continued to live with her from time to time, but his visits became less and less frequent. Still the promises persisted. Everything would work out. He'd get his divorce and he and Debbie would be married.

Married? she kept asking herself. *When?*

The doctor began exerting pressure for a partial payment on her medical expenses, but her man came through with nothing. Debbie could barely afford to meet her day-to-day living expenses without the added costs the child would bring. Then early in the last month of her pregnancy, her man disappeared. He wasn't to be found anywhere.

She made anonymous calls to his wife and to his employer, but the answer was always the same. He was gone, left without telling anyone, and no one knew where he was. His employer had already replaced him with another driver. His wife was frantic. She was obviously still in love with him and could not understand his strange behavior in recent weeks. She indicated to Debbie that he was always a good husband and provider and this unexplainable disappearance was something she could not fathom.

Debbie's mental stress was almost more than she could bear. Her hopes had been dashed to pieces by the false promises of a man who had deserted her in the final and critical stages of her pregnancy.

Her finances were virtually exhausted. Her landlord would not accept promises for apartment rent, and the doctor wanted his fees—preferably before the baby was delivered.

Debbie contemplated suicide and took what she thought was an overdose of sleeping pills one night. The dosage, however, was not large enough to do any permanent damage. All it did was make her terribly sick.

She had not been a resident of the state or county long enough to qualify for welfare. She might've gone to one of the churches, but without any religious background or training she didn't know upon which door to knock. There was one last hope: the police.

"In the eyes of some," she said frankly, "the police might be called PIGS, but I've come to know some of them at the truck stop and they aren't the monsters people make them out to be."

"Reverend," she went on, "my baby's due any day now, and I just don't know what to do. I'm broke, and my man has gone. What do I do about the baby? I'm not sure that I can afford to keep it once it's born."

"Debbie, let's think about the possibilities you have," I said. "Your man is gone. He skipped out because he didn't want to assume the moral obligations of the act or to incur any financial responsibility toward this child. I don't see any help for you at all from him. We can scratch him."

"Yes, sir, I guess you're right about that." I could tell by the way she said it that she had already come to that conclusion on her own.

"We've got two other possible alternatives," I said, "and both are very real. You can keep this child once it is born, or you can place it for adoption. There is no ideal answer or solution. Either way you go, there will be problems. Keeping the baby has certain complications, and placing it up for adoption presents others. Let's evaluate this if we can.

"You *can* keep the baby, but that will mean returning to work much sooner than you should for your own physical safety. The baby must be cared for while you work—which means additional expense. A child needs the love and affection that only a mother can give. Keeping the baby may seem wonderful right now, but project into the future if you can. Think about the child.

"I believe your man is gone for good. You will fall in love again, and someday you will marry. Is it going to be fair to your future husband to bring an illegitimate child into his life? Will he be big enough to understand?

"You see, Debbie," I continued, "these are very real questions, and I want you to try to understand the seriousness of the responsibilities you must assume if you elect to keep this child."

"I just don't know. I just don't know what to do, Reverend," she whispered, twisting a sodden handkerchief between her fingers.

"There's more to be considered, Debbie. I'm asking now if you could put the child up for adoption. Again, this isn't easy, but I'm asking you to think about it as a possibility." I didn't want to make her unhappy, but thought it best to talk the problem through before we stopped.

"There are advantages for you and the baby. It will solve your financial stress and strain, since the adoptive parents would pay your doctor and hospital bills. We can be reasonably sure the baby will be placed with parents who will be able to provide for its physical and financial needs. Also, the child will receive a mother's and father's care and love as it grows and develops. Adoptive parents, I've learned, look upon their children as if they had been their own offspring. You could feel assured that your baby was in a loving home with a desirable environment and surroundings. You couldn't ask for anything better than that—"

"I know," she nodded, "but I'm not sure. This is my child and I don't know if I can bear to give him away—" Her voice faltered.

"Look, Debbie, I'm not asking you to make a decision tonight. You're tired, you're upset, and you're unable to think clearly. You need help with your decision—a higher help than I can give you. Debbie, do you believe in God?"

"God?" she queried. "Yes, I think I do, but I'm not sure about Him. Why do you ask?"

"I ask, Debbie, because He's all that's left. You've got to take this problem to Him and let Him help you wrestle with it. I'll respect your decision once it's made, if you let God help you make it. I'll be praying for you as you pray about it. When the answer comes, it will be the right answer—this much I can promise.

"The day after tomorrow is Sunday. I don't know if you've ever set foot in a church before in your life. But I want you to come Sunday morning. It doesn't matter what you wear or how you look. Just come. We're only a few blocks from where you are living, and if you can't walk we'll arrange to get you there. Pray about this tonight, pray tomorrow, and come on Sunday morning and pray again. It'll make a difference. You're going to get your answer; I know you will."

Debbie came to church on Sunday. I saw her sitting in one of the back pews alone with her head bowed most of the hour.

Maybe she didn't know what it was all about, but she had come, and in her own way she was praying to God and laying her problem upon Him where it belonged. She was waiting at my study door after the service.

"May I speak with you a moment?" she asked.

Once inside the study she told me how for the first time in her life something strange, mysterious, and wonderful had happened.

"There is a God," she said. "I felt Him and heard Him speaking this morning. I looked at the stained-glass window and saw Jesus carrying the baby lamb in His arms, and knew that if He cared about a lamb, He cared about me. Jesus has lifted my burden. I think I know what I must do, but I need to pray some more about it. Will you pray with me before I leave?"

Debbie and I prayed. As she left the study she turned to say that she would be back the next morning with her decision.

I had to ask God to allow me to give Debbie the support and encouragement she needed whatever her decision might be.

She showed up Monday morning—early! Once in the study she suddenly lost all control of her emotions and began crying like a baby.

"Debbie," I asked, "are you all right? Do you want to talk now or would you like to wait until later?"

"I'll be all right in a minute. It's just . . ." her voice trailed off. "It's just that it's so hard for me to tell you. I've made a decision and want to believe it's right."

Slowly her sobbing subsided, then her head dropped, and I knew she was asking God for strength for the moment. I bowed my head in silence, too.

"Mr. Asmuth, I hope you'll understand," she said finally. "This baby is part of me. He's inside of me right now, and I can feel him. He's alive, and I'm his mother. Do you understand how I feel?" she said.

"I understand, Debbie," I said, crestfallen because I thought she had decided to keep the baby. *What kind of life could it have?*

"I want to keep this baby, Mr. Asmuth," Debbie continued. "I'm the mother, and every woman wants to bear children and raise a family. I want to keep this baby—but I can't. Not with a clear conscience. It wouldn't be fair." I hoped she didn't notice my sigh of relief. She was shaking her head as she went on. "A child needs two parents—a mother and a father. I'm only half the team. What I *want* to do and what I *can* do are two different things." Debbie was trying to smile. "I kept hearing this voice, a voice that kept saying, 'You've got to give the baby up, Debbie, you've got to give him up.' I heard it every time I prayed, and I believe this is what God wants me to do—because it's best for the baby and best for me.

"It was a terrible decision to make, Mr. Asmuth," she said. "But I know we've both got a chance this way. You promised the baby would get a good home, and this is awfully important to me. And I can start all over again and maybe someday fall in love with a man who wants me as his wife and the mother of our children. I'm going to be a good mother the next time." She paused a moment and then added, "Tell me I've done the right thing. Tell me that I have!"

"God doesn't lead us in wrong directions," I told Debbie. "Often we either don't listen carefully enough or just fail to heed what He seems to be suggesting. If you feel this is what God is leading you to do, you're doing the right thing. And He will lead you through the days ahead if you place your hand in His." Inwardly I prayed my own thanksgiving.

"What do we do now?" she asked. "Where do we go from here?"

Whatever I did had to be done thoughtfully, thoroughly, and quickly. It was going to take some cooperation from doctors and a lawyer. *Could we come through on time?* I was asking myself. I knew that we must for Debbie's sake and for the sake of the baby.

"There's one more thing, Debbie, something you've got to know," I said, not wanting to keep anything from her. "You will legally sign this baby over, through an attorney, before he is born. This means that you will never see the baby. You won't know whether you had a boy or a girl, and you won't know who the adoptive parents are. This may sound cruel, but it's done for your protection and that of the baby and the adoptive parents."

Debbie bordered on tears again, but held them back. In a barely audible whisper she said, "I realize this. It's just that it's hard—" She turned her head to hide the tears and went on her way, raising her hand in a simple gesture of good-bye.

I had my work cut out when Debbie left the study. I first tried two adoption agencies—no luck. They couldn't possibly accept a baby on such short notice. Usually I have the names of some families who want babies, but this time I had none. The only thing to do was try some of my doctor friends. I hit the jackpot with the first call. This doctor, a great guy and a Christian, understood the problem. He happened to know a wonderful family who loved kids, were unable to have any more of their own and yet wanted another.

"I'll make a few phone calls and be in touch before noon today," he promised, "but you've got a family for this baby."

There were a lot of little details, but they were all handled in short order, and this phase of Debbie's problem was solved. There was an emotional after-birth upheaval, but this was faced and she came through it all very well.

She recovered fast, and was released from the hospital looking like a new woman. There was a radiance in her face that I had never seen before. I knew she had been praying, and that God had lifted her burden. She might not have accepted Jesus as Savior and Lord, but that moment was coming.

"I hate to be so much trouble to you," she said as she visited again in my study, "but can you help me again?"

"If it's possible, Debbie," I assured her. "If not, I'll try to find someone who will."

"I want to leave this town," she said. "I want to get out and go somewhere—make a new beginning. I'm going to talk to the doctor and ask how soon I can travel. I'll leave as soon as he releases me. Do you think," she asked, "that you can help me get a new job?"

I knew my chances for getting her employment were better locally because of my contacts, but I could appreciate her reasons for wanting to settle somewhere else.

"Debbie, could you move to the Florida east coast?" I asked. "I've got some contacts in the Miami-Fort Lauderdale area."

"I'll go anywhere, just so I get out of this town," she said. I detected a certain bitterness, but this was natural when everything you've ever wanted and hoped for has been shattered and destroyed.

"Debbie," I promised, "when you're ready we'll get you to the other side of the state, find a place for you to stay, put a little money in your pocket, and line up some job possibilities. How does that sound?" I asked her.

"No one could ask for more than that," she replied, shook my hand confidently, and went on her way.

God, I said after she left, *how do I get into these predicaments? I've promised that girl the moon, and I don't even know if I have enough money in my "slush fund" for the bus ticket to Miami. I told Debbie to put her trust in You, and I guess I better really believe now, too.*

Thank God for Christian friends! A fellow pastor on the opposite side of the state was able to line up housing for Debbie, and offered several prospects for employment.

With Debbie reestablished in a new area, her life had new

meaning. I made her promise when she left that she would keep up her worship at church in her new home. Later I learned that she had confessed Christ as her Lord, and was like a new person. *God, You've done it again through the transforming power of Christ when He enters a person's life,* I thought to myself. *Maybe You sent Debbie to the police station that night several weeks ago—I'm glad You did.*

IX. FEUDIN' AND FUSSIN'

To the married I give charge . . . that the wife should not separate from her husband . . . (I Cor. 7:10).

"Rev, do you know a Mary Lipton out on Bonita Street?" the desk sergeant asked.

"I sure do, Sarge," I said with real emphasis; "she's bad news. I've lost count of the number of times I've been to that house. Are they at it again?"

"I don't know what they're doing or what's going on, but there was a lot of commotion in the background over the phone. Kids were screaming—sounded like a dozen of 'em—and a man was cussing and fussing at her all the while she talked. She was desperate, and asked specifically that we send you."

"It isn't going to be pretty," I said to the lieutenant, "but let's get with it."

As we walked out the door toward the car, I half-seriously and half-jokingly turned to the sergeant and said, "Sarge, better have a couple of cells ready. We may need them before we're through with these mavericks tonight!"

"Rev, what's this all about?" the lieutenant said as we started down the road. "Do you want the red lights and siren?"

"Loot, you're in for an experience if you haven't met Mary Lipton. No red lights and siren, just take your time. Maybe it'll be all over when we arrive. It's like I told the Sarge, they're bad news!

"I met Mary on the night of a near tragedy, Loot," I explained . . .

It was Easter, and I received an anonymous call that a woman was trying to commit suicide. The station called me on my car radio, but I was several miles out of the city and knew it would take some time to get to the scene. Two uniformed men arrived first. When I pulled up they were all standing outside where a heated conversation was in progress between the lawmen and a lean lanky man who looked like he had tangled with a wildcat. His clothes were torn to shreds. Four small children were wandering aimlessly around the front yard. An assortment of neighbors was standing at a safe distance in the adjoining yards.

"Look, Butch," one of our men was saying, "suppose you explain to the Reverend here what you've been telling us."

I was close enough to know that Butch had been drinking. His speech was slurred, his stance unsteady, and he was overly aggressive. He was also talkative. The neighborhood spectators had box seats as Butch's fragmented story came through loudly.

"Reverend," Butch almost shouted, "Mary's pregnant! She's in labor right now inside that house and won't let anyone near her. She shot at me three times tonight, then threw herself on the floor trying to kill the baby. She's still got the gun."

"Are you Mary's husband?" I asked Butch.

There was silence, then the sheepish reply, "No, we're not married. We've been living together. I've been paying the bills, and I fathered this child, but we're not married. She doesn't want my baby. She wants to kill it, and will kill me too if she can. Look at me, Reverend." He indicated his ripped-apart shirt. "That woman has torn me up. And you oughta see the inside of that house! She wanted to move out earlier tonight and take the four kids with her. When I tried to stop her, she ripped up everything I own. I don't have a single thing she hasn't torn up. I can't even go to work in the morning 'cause I got nothing left to wear. That woman is crazy, Reverend—she's out of her mind."

"What about these other four kids, Butch? Are they yours and hers or what?" I asked.

"No sir, they ain't mine. All four of those children got different fathers, and she wasn't married to anybody when she had 'em. Some she married—yeah, I guess she married all four of 'em later. But none of 'em lasted. She was married to some other guy when we started running around, but that's over now. I want to marry her, but she'll have nothing more to do with me. She wants to see me dead. She'll do it, Reverend—that woman'll put a bullet right between my eyes."

"Do you think Mary will talk with me?" I asked. He looked at me like he thought I was crazy.

"You can try. She wouldn't let any of these cops near her though. They all got as far as the bedroom door, and she just held that gun on 'em until they backed out. I'm afraid someone's gonna get killed."

I could hear some profane garbling intermingled with threats coming from the house. This really wasn't attempted suicide—it was just a complicated lovers' squabble.

"Butch," I said, moving toward the house, "you stay out here. If Mary's in labor, I've got to talk her into going to the hospital. I also want that gun before someone gets killed. We'll worry about your personal problems later."

The detective walked ahead of me. He was thinking that perhaps I could gain admission to the bedroom, relieve her of the weapon, and persuade her to go to the hospital. But it wasn't that easy. Brandishing a five-shot snub-nosed revolver, Mary cursed at us and warned us to stay where we were.

I could understand why men were attracted to Mary. She was very pretty and well proportioned, a fact which even her pregnancy could not hide. *No wonder Butch is so infatuated with her,* I thought.

"Mary, I'm not going to harm you, I won't take your gun. Just let me talk to you." I took a tentative step forward.

"One step through that door and there'll be a bullet through you," she retorted.

"Pull the trigger if you want, but I'm coming in," I said, edging through the doorway and moving cautiously toward her.

She was sitting on the edge of the bed, the gun pointed straight at my midsection. I didn't *think* she would shoot, but I was determined to get to her whatever the risk.

I made it! I sat gingerly down beside her on the bed. The gun was still pointed straight ahead, and she was staring away from me.

"The pains, Mary, how are the pains?" I asked.

"Never you worry about the pains. I'm all right. I just hope I killed this bastard baby when I pounded my stomach on that hardwood floor. I want it to die! And I don't want to see Butch again," she said bitterly. "Just get him out of here and leave me alone."

"It's not your decision to make, Mary, as to whether the baby lives or dies. You can keep it or give it away, but you don't have the right to kill the baby or yourself," I warned. "Why don't you let us get you to the hospital so you can see a doctor?"

"I ain't seen no doctor yet, and there's no sense in goin' now. I'm gonna have this—" She was interrupted by the sound of a crashing, splintering door.

There was no time for thought. Butch had charged into the

house, thrown a shoulder block at the detective standing at the door, and was hurtling into the bedroom toward Mary. She raised the gun and I lurched, throwing her off balance. She fired twice, the gun going off like an explosion. Both shots went into the ceiling. Regaining her balance she pointed the gun again and pulled the trigger. The hammer clicked sharply —the gun was empty! By this time the detective had Butch in a hammerlock, and I had the gun. They dragged Butch from the house. Outside I could hear Butch shouting that he was coming back in. Mary was screaming from the bedroom that she was not going to the hospital and that she was going to kill Butch. I knew that as long as Butch was mouthing off outside I'd never get Mary calmed down enough to do any serious reasoning with her.

"Mary," I said, "I'm stepping outside for a few minutes to talk to Butch. You lie there and do a little picking at your conscience. I can't make you go to the hospital, but your life is involved. What's it worth?"

I turned and quickly walked to the front of the house where Butch was still trying to convince the officers that he was really a solid man, that he never touched booze, and that he was vitally interested in Mary's welfare.

"Look, you guys, just let me go back and talk with her," he was pleading.

"You heard that woman," the officer said. "She doesn't want anything to do with you. You can either get in your car and leave, or we'll provide you with lodging for the next several days!"

"Listen here, man," Butch said abruptly, "I pay the rent on this place. I buy the groceries. I ain't goin' nowhere. You understand? I ain't leavin' this house. Not now or ever!"

"Okay, Butch," I said as I walked up, "so you pay the rent and buy the groceries. But you've had too much to drink, and Mary's in no shape to think about much except that baby which she doesn't want. Just do as you've been told and leave!"

"You guys are making a big mistake," he argued. "I'll leave, but only because I don't want to spend the night in jail. You haven't heard the last of this. I'll be back."

"Butch, just go," I said. "We'll talk about it in the morning. You call me then, and things may look different to everyone."

He stormed off to the car, slammed the door closed, and took off down the road in a state of rage. I had a feeling I would see him again before the night was over.

The children, who had witnessed the whole thing, were trembling with fear. I went back to the bedroom for more talking with Mary.

"We've sent Butch off for the night," I said. "Let's forget about him for now, and think about you and the baby. You've got to go to the hospital. You're in labor—you know what's going to happen."

"What about my children?" she asked, more reasonable now that Butch was gone. "Who'll take care of them? Someone has to look after 'em while I'm gone."

"I'll have one of the men call the children's home, Mary," I said. "Perhaps we can get them in there tonight. They'll be well cared for and can stay at the home while you are in the hospital."

She seemed suddenly agreeable, and I called for one of the men to make contact with the home and determine the availability of space for a few days.

As we were all leaving the house my detective friend, Harold Ford, said, "Preach, you take Mary to the hospital in her car. I'll meet you there." With that he loaded the four kids in his car and disappeared down the road into the darkness. I was left standing by Mary's car, trying to figure out how to get a pregnant woman in labor squeezed into a car that was packed from floorboards to ceiling with all of her personal belongings.

The car was a fifty-dollar casket on wheels, a real piece of junk. Finally, I managed to get Mary in on one side, and I sandwiched myself in on the other.

Cautiously I eased out of the driveway. The rearview mirror was useless because of all the stuff piled in the back seat. *I'll trust the Lord to get Mary to the hospital before the baby comes,* I thought. By then it was 2:00 A.M. and the streets were empty.

All went well until we came to the first stop sign and my foot hit the brake pedal. It went all the way to the floorboard and the car just sailed right on through the intersection without even slowing down.

"Oh, I forgot to tell you, Mr. Reverend," Mary said. "This car doesn't have no brakes. You'll just have to drive a little slower and be more careful when you come to the stop signs."

"I'll keep that in mind," I said, slowing down to a creep.

Mary's frame of mind had improved. "You're a preacher, aren't you?" she asked. "You saved me from killing Butch and have taken care of my kids. Maybe the church isn't as bad as I thought it was. Maybe people do care about others. When I was a girl I just stopped going to church. I wasn't wanted or welcome. They called me a little whore behind my back, and maybe I was. Tell me, Reverend, do you think that God can love someone like me?"

"Funny thing about God, Mary," I said. "He doesn't care who we are or what we have or what we've done. He loves us and will forgive us and will help us change our ways."

The Holy Spirit had opened the door for me and seemed to be providing a way to reach this woman's heart. Then Satan interfered. The red temperature gauge on the dashboard lit up, and at the same time I noticed smoke pouring from under the hood. Before I could react, the car sputtered to a halt in the middle of an intersection on the main street through town. What a spot to be in!

"Something else I forgot to tell you," she said, shrugging her shoulders. "The radiator has a leak. We should have put water in it before we left the house."

I groaned inwardly. There was a long period of silence as we sat there, stalled in the middle of the street.

Then Mary said, "Reverend, the pains are harder. I think the baby's coming."

God, I prayed silently, *I've got a problem. I'm no doctor and a pretty poor midwife. Please, help!*

I had visions, horrible visions, of trying to deliver a baby in the middle of the night in the middle of the street.

A telephone, I thought. *I've got to find a telephone! I've got to call the station and have them send a car.*

The old law applies to preachers as well as other sinners: when you need a policeman, you can't find him. The downtown cars were probably busy in the area checking doors. They were not in sight.

"The baby's coming!" Mary wailed.

"Just sit tight," I said desperately. "I'm running to that pay phone in the next block to call the station for another car. Be right back." I sprinted toward the phone booth.

"Send me a car—any car—to Tenth and Iris Streets—quick. This woman is having a baby in the middle of the street." I hung up and dashed back to Mary.

Moments later the cruiser arrived. I escorted Mary from her piece of junk and instructed the officer to get her to the hospital fast!

"And have the station try to find that detective who deserted me," I shouted as he pulled away.

A laughing Harold Ford with four children in his car soon appeared.

"What's the trouble, Preach, doesn't anyone love you?" He grinned at me.

"Help me push this bomb over to the curb, and then get me

some water," I said disgustedly. "I'll drive it to the city lot and lock it up if you promise not to let me out of your sight the rest of the night."

The car was soon taken care of. We reluctantly left the children with responsible adults in the children's home. As we drove away we received a call on the radio.

"Butch is at the emergency room giving the attendants a bad time," the dispatcher said.

The scene in the emergency room was one of big-lip Butch telling the officers who had arrived before us what he was and was not going to do. I knew what Butch was going to do—he was going to spend the night in jail. He did!

I learned later that same night that Mary's baby had been born dead. I tried, before she left the hospital, and several times after, to reach her for God. But I just wasn't getting through. Something in her background or some earlier unpleasant experience with religion had soured her beyond help. Nothing I said seemed to soak in. Now the lieutenant and I were on our way out to Mary's house again. Would it be more of the same old story?

"Lieutenant," I said as we drove toward Mary's house, "I don't think she is totally lost or hopeless; it's just that I can't seem to reach her. It's so futile. She's still letting Butch live with her, off and on. In her own way she seems to be a good mother to the children, but Butch keeps the water stirred up all the time.

"I've suggested she pack up and leave the city, start fresh someplace else, but still she stays. I've invited her to church, given her a Bible and some guidance in how to read it, but nothing happens. So, there's no telling what we'll find tonight."

"What do you want us to do, Rev?" he asked.

"Just be there, ready to move in if I need you," I answered.

We could hear the battle noises as we nosed the car into the drive. Another cruiser pulled in right behind us. I knocked on the door, but couldn't be heard above the shouting and cursing. I pushed the door open and gingerly stepped inside.

The place was a shambles. Mary and Butch were not even aware I was inside, and I found myself ducking their flying missiles being hurled across the room. Everything in the house was broken. Drunken New Year's Eve revelers couldn't have done this well. Men's, women's, and children's clothing was strewn all about, completely torn to shreds. Everything was literally ripped to pieces. Broken glass and splintered furniture lay all over the house, in a fog of the most abusive language I'd ever heard. These two had really declared war, and there were no signs of either raising the white flag of surrender.

"Hey, are you two idiots trying to kill each other?" I shouted, taking them by surprise.

They both froze, dropped what they were holding, and started shouting at me at the same time. Each tried to explain what had happened, while sparring verbally with each other.

"Okay, stop this foolishness," I heard the lieutenant bark behind me, "or we'll lock you both up!" But they paid no attention to him.

The lieutenant and I walked toward Mary, while two other uniformed men went for Butch. Both were good and mad, and it took some time to cool them down so we could piece the whole fracas together.

Mary had ordered Butch out and out for good. He came home from work while she was out for the evening and found his belongings on the front porch. Incensed, he moved them back in and decided that since he was footing the bills it was his house just as much as it was hers. He was going to stay.

Mary came home, found Butch and his belongings in the house, and the volcano erupted. Mary went for Butch's things and with surgical precision proceeded to cut, tear, and destroy. Not to be outdone, Butch did the same thing with Mary's clothing and the children's. And the brawl was on.

We quieted them down, but neither was going to leave the house, each trying to outwit the other. Neither one of them would be reasonable, and we couldn't baby-sit with the two of them for the rest of the night. Perhaps in the morning I could get this resolved, but not tonight.

Both were advised of the availability of a warrant, and strangely enough each took out a warrant against the other.

A neighbor offered to take the children for the night, and when we got Mary and Butch to the station the warrants were served. Neither had enough money to put up the bail bond, so they willingly went to jail, each feeling the other got precisely what he deserved. With Mary and Butch in the city's "tender-loving-care" for the night, the lieutenant and I left the station.

"I see what you mean about their being 'bad news,' Rev," the lieutenant said. "That house looked worse than a bar after a knife fight. That Mary is a little spitfire if I ever saw one. What are you going to do with this twosome when they are released?"

"I don't know, Loot, I just don't know. Somewhere there's an answer. Beneath her veneer Mary's a genuine person who wants to do right, but every time she tries, our society kicks her in the teeth. But, if God said something about 'seventy times seven' this means that I've just got to keep trying. It's just that it takes longer with some than it does with others."

"Would you believe 'never' with some, Rev?" the lieutenant asked hesitantly.

"No, sir, I would not believe that. We just haven't opened the right door for either of them. I know they're bad news, but God can and does change people, and I know that in His providence He can change Mary and Butch."

My little sermon was interrupted by the radio. "Car four, go to 1576 Chili Avenue. Attempted suicide. There's another car standing by at the scene."

"10–4, we're 10–51, 1576 Chili Avenue," I said, hanging up the mike. In a city that seems to never sleep there's always something happening.

"Car nine to car four," we heard on the radio.

"Four, go ahead," I was quick to answer.

"Car four, you better hurry. She isn't dead but we can't get to her without the risk of her following through on her threat," the voice said.

"10–4, car nine, we're coming down the street now," I said, and then checked us out at the scene with the station.

X. SUICIDE ANNIE

. . . *the Lord gave, and the Lord has taken away* (Job 1:21).

One look at the house and I knew where we were. The address was a familiar number in the complaint logs. Police cars with red lights penetrating the night's darkness act like rotten beef attracting maggots. People seem to come from everywhere. This could be none other than the infamous Annie!

A black officer met me at the front door of the house—an unsafe wood frame home that dated back to the turn of the century. Doors were loosely hung, window panes were broken, and the front porch was in a state of dry rot and might collapse if you stepped too heavily upon it. The peeling paint added to the shabby look of the dwelling.

"Rev," the officer said, "you've got a bad one. We've tried everything, but she won't let us in the bedroom. The closest we can get is the door. One step further and she threatens to jab that knife blade closer to the jugular vein."

The house inside was utter filth and stench, mixed with an assortment of emotionally distressed people who must have crawled out of the woodwork. Clutter was everywhere, and the reek of cheap whiskey. I motioned to two of the other uniformed men who were already in the house to remove some of the people who were adding to the confusion and tension. They got the message and moved with dispatch.

The black officer directed me toward a dark hallway, with a dim light breaking into the darkness from a room at the end. The two of us walked quietly down the hall, followed by another uniformed man. A cursory glance into the room conveyed the message. We'd had Annie several times before on the usual things—drunk, disorderly conduct, shoplifting, disturbance, even assault and battery. Never, though, did I think that Annie would come to this.

She was lying naked on the bed. Annie had been an attractive girl in her earlier years, but fast living and hard liquor were beginning to show. She looked several years older than her forty years. A faint trickle of blood traced an erratic path down the side of her neck, ending with a steady drip, drip, drip in a widening pool of redness on the soiled sheet beneath her. Labored breathing, a trembling body, and eyes that were glazed, glassy, staring off into space, told the story. Clutched tightly in her hand was a glistening, well-honed, twelve-inch knife with its tip pressing ever-so-gently against her jugular vein. The point had only lightly penetrated the skin and the bleeding was not bad—yet. Alongside the bottle on the bedside table was a well-thumbed Bible. Annie was drunk, desperate, and dangerous, and the wrong move by any one of us might cause the fatal thrust of the knife deep into her throat.

The gap separating us was too wide for any attempt at a foolish move. Even in her sluggish, drunken stupor she could shove the knife. *You can't rush,* I was thinking, *or Annie's name will be in tomorrow's obituary column.*

"Annie, will you talk to me?" I asked without the slightest display of emotion in my voice. "There are better answers to your problems than that knife you hold in your hand."

"Reverend, you take one mo' step through that door and it's gonna be me or you," she said. "Don't tempt me, Reverend. I'll do it if I has to."

It all came out in a drunken slur, but I knew she meant it. "I won't come in, Annie, but I do want to talk. Before you do something to hurt your kinfolk in the living room, Annie, won't you talk with me?" I asked.

"You can do all your talkin' a-standin' by that door, Reverend. I might do a little listenin' but you ain't gonna stop me from killin' myself!" Annie said.

"I've got one question, Annie, just one," I said. "Why do you want to die?"

"There's nothin' mo' to live for. I'm tired of livin'. I reckon I just got the blahs." With her free hand she reached for the vodka bottle, taking a swig big enough to floor the average drinker.

Wait until that hits the blood stream, I thought. *She'll either have all the courage she needs or she'll pass out.*

She placed the bottle back on the nightstand and wiped her lips with her arm saying, "I thought you wanted to talk to me, Reverend. I'm still waitin' to hear you say somethin'!"

"Annie, let's talk about that Bible by the bottle. I'd like to believe it was you who read it. It's been used a lot. Its pages are worn and the binding is broken. Have you done all the reading in that book, Annie?" I asked.

"I've read that book from one end to the other more than once," she acknowledged. Then she boasted, "I knows all about it, maybe even more'n some of you preachers."

"What does it say about killing in the Bible, Annie?" I asked her.

"It says in the Ten Commandments, 'Thou shalt not kill,' but I ain't killed nobody. I'm just fixin' to kill myself."

"It says 'kill,' Annie, and when God said, 'Thou shalt not kill,' He included YOU in that commandment. You don't have any right to take your own life. Things may be bad like you said, and you may have the blahs, but God even has a cure for that."

"I loves my little chillun, but it's my man what gives me the blahs. He's a runner," she said.

"He's a what?" I asked.

"A runner. Ain't you never heard of a runner, Reverend? He runs from one woman to another. All those people out there carryin' on 'bout poor ol' Annie, but you ain't seen my husband, has you? No, suh, 'cause he ain't there. He's in some other woman's bed right now."

I could tell the last swig of liquor was taking effect.

"Annie," I said, "I'm leaving. We're all leaving. You just go ahead and do whatever you want to do."

"You're all chicken, that's what you is. I'm gonna kill myself, just you wait 'n see . . ." Her voice trailed off as we turned and walked away.

Once back in the living room the lieutenant threw me one of his skeptical glances. "Think about how you're going to feel if Annie kills herself while we're having a tea party in the living room, Rev," he said. "One of us ought to be back there keeping an eye on that woman—she's desperate."

"She's drunk, Lieutenant, and we both know it," I replied. "Annie isn't going to kill herself or anyone else. We'll wait ten minutes, and I'll go back to the room. Everything is going to turn out just fine. I'm sure of it." *At least, I hope so*, I said to myself.

"Rev, you better be right," the Loot continued. He didn't look too sure about it.

"Just relax, Loot. All I'm asking for is ten minutes, and we'll be on our way." The lieutenant wasn't convinced, but he was game and went along with my request.

The family was no problem; all they needed was a little reassurance. They believed, but Loot was still in a doubting mood.

Annie, I thought, *how many more like you are there that we have tried to salvage down through the years, and how many more yet to come? All have been emotionally disturbed and couldn't face reality; they've just given up. I don't know why, Annie, but you want to give up, too.*

Waiting for Annie to cool off and realize there was no answer in suicide, I stepped out on the porch to get alone with God and pray. There, in the still night air, I remembered another suicide attempt—and took heart.

I had been called at home one night about midnight by a man staying in a local motel.

"I'm going to commit suicide, and you'll find me in this room," he said. "Be here in ten minutes or you'll find me dead. And don't call the cops."

I had only enough time to call my associate minister, Lee Laack, and ask him to meet me at the motel. Two heads would be better than one, I figured. I radioed the police station, briefly stated what I was doing, and asked them to send a car if they didn't hear from me within an hour. I knew that sometimes innocent people have been killed just before the other fellow commits suicide. One thing I've learned as a preacher-policeman is to take no unnecessary chances.

Lee was waiting at the motel when I arrived. We knocked and the door was opened. A nice looking middle-aged man politely invited us in.

"I'm Barney," he said. "I want to leave three notes with you before I end it. Then you men are going to watch me die."

Barney handed us the notes. One was to his estranged wife, one to his children, and the other to the police department. In the letter to the police department he apologized for the inconvenience he had caused and gave instructions on how to notify his next of kin.

In the note to his children he told of his love, explained how he had tried to be a good father, but had failed to keep their mother happy. Again, he apologized profusely for hurting them in this way, but said he knew of nothing else to do.

The long letter to his wife was full of bitterness. He spoke of his inability to keep her sexually satisfied, and his failure to provide for her exorbitant material demands. He knew she no longer loved him, but he loved her very much and this estrangement was breaking his heart. If he couldn't have her, he didn't want to go on living.

His notes indicated that he was well educated but had fallen to the bottom of the heap. He had been running for weeks, and was registered in the motel under an alias.

I glanced around the room, but could see no evidence of a suicide weapon. No knife, gun, nor pills.

"Reverend," Barney said, "I was once an elder in the Presbyterian church. We were good church people, went every Sunday and took the kids to Sunday school. But I was under pressure in my work. I was a traveling salesman, made good money, but was gone several weeks every month. I didn't want it that way, but I had to keep on the move to keep the money coming in. I guess that's when it started to happen. My wife just lost interest in me and started taking up with these other guys.

"When I walked in one Friday night and she told me it was all over, I went to pieces. She told me the divorce papers would be served Monday morning. I loved that woman, honest I did. And those children—there wasn't anything I wouldn't do for them. But now it's all over. If I've hurt them I'm sorry, but this is the end of the line for me. I'm jumping off!"

"Okay, Barney," I said, "but if it's all over, why did you call us? Why didn't you just do the job and let us sleep? I don't think that you'll go through with it, at least not tonight." I hoped I was on the right track, trying to call his bluff.

Lee and I both sat there watching his every move. Suddenly he stood up and moved toward the bathroom. I started to follow, but he turned on me and my heart sank into my shoes.

"Don't make any false moves, Reverend," he said with determination. "I'm bigger than both of you guys, and you aren't going to stop me. Just sit down and watch."

He disappeared into the bathroom, but emerged within seconds holding a water glass filled with a bilious-looking liquid. The smell of the concoction—even from across the room—was enough to make me nauseated. He stood in the doorway holding the glass.

"Remember what I told you guys," he said. "Don't try and stop me or I'll flatten both of you. It won't take long. I'll down this, and in a matter of minutes it will be all over. You can call an ambulance when I fall in a heap and begin wallowing on the floor, but by the time they get me to the hospital I'll be dead."

It was a cruel thing for me to say, but I had nothing to lose. I leaned back in the chair and said, "Go ahead and drink that foul-smelling thing. I want you to get the job over with so I can go back to bed. Got a big day coming up tomorrow." I opened my mouth and faked a yawn.

It was just the shocker he needed. He placed the glass on the washstand and stood glaring at me. Slowly he entered the main part of the room and sat on the edge of the bed.

"You don't want me to do it, do you, Reverend?" he said.

"Don't want you to do what, Barney?" I answered, trying to seem disinterested.

"You don't want me to take my life," he replied, almost as if he was wanting to persuade me.

"Look, Barney, I don't like to see people kill themselves. No matter what the problem is, there are better answers than suicide. Perhaps you've been trying to go it alone—but we're never really alone. If you're a Presbyterian elder as you said, then some of the church's teachings should have rubbed off on you by now. But I can't stop you. If you want to drink your poison, go ahead. Suicide isn't the answer, however," I said matter-of-factly.

"Then what is the answer?" he almost shouted.

"Barney, on the nightstand by the bed is a Gideon Bible. If you'll hand it to me I'll read you a couple of passages. Sure, you've heard them before, but it might do you good to hear them again."

Suspiciously he reached for the Bible. I turned to the book of Psalms. I read first from the 46th Psalm, giving particular emphasis to the words, "God is our refuge and strength, a very present help in trouble. Therefore will not we fear, though the earth be removed . . ." Then, I flashed back to the 121st Psalm and those reassuring words, "I will lift up mine eyes unto the hills, from whence cometh my help. My help cometh from the Lord, which made heaven and earth. He will not suffer thy foot to be moved: he that keepeth thee will not slumber . . ."

He sat in complete silence without visible change in his emotions. I'd have to try something else.

"Barney," I said, "you know the Shepherd's Psalm, the 23rd, but I'm going to read it again so those words can sink in." When I finished, the three of us sat in silence for a long while.

Barney finally broke the silence by asking, "What time are your services in the morning?"

"They're at nine and eleven," Lee said. "Would you like to join us for worship?"

There was no reply. He walked again to the bathroom while we both watched nervously. For a long time he stood looking at his glass of poison, then tipped it and poured it down the sink. I didn't know what Barney was going to do tomorrow, but I did know he wasn't going to die tonight.

He looked like a new man when he came out of that bathroom. He had found peace with God. He took the suicide notes and tore them in pieces, then let them fall from his hands to the wastebasket.

"I guess you can go now. You'll see me in the morning at one of those services," he said. "I know I don't have all the answers, but I do remember something that Jesus said: 'Him that cometh to me I will in no wise cast out.' I've got to begin making a new life for myself, and that's going to mean starting all over. I know, now, that God will help me do it."

We shook hands with Barney and departed relieved. What could have been a bad scene, fortunately had a happy ending. Barney was in church the next morning, called me later in the day and left town on Monday. I never knew what became of him, but somehow I believe God used us to help guide Barney through the blackest night of his life.

I inhaled deeply as I thanked God for His ability to save and walked back into Annie's house. The lieutenant followed me down the hall, and we looked in Annie's room where she was sound asleep in a drunken stupor, still holding onto the knife.

Quietly I entered the room, and finger by finger broke the grip she now had on the knife. Within seconds it was in my hand, not Annie's. I pulled the bed sheet up to cover her naked frame, turned out the lamp on the nightstand and left the room.

An amazed lieutenant was standing in the doorway shaking his head.

"You were just lucky, Rev," he said, "that she didn't wake up when you tried to get that knife and cut you to pieces."

"It wasn't luck, Loot," I said. "Someone was watching over me. Annie's world is going to look a lot better in the morning when she has slept off this nightmare. Here, you can have the knife."

As the two of us walked down the hall, we passed the black officer who had been with us. Loot handed him the knife, saying, "You can have this as a souvenir of Rev's lucky night!"

"Car four, 10–19. We've got a man at the desk that just gave the sergeant a gun saying he almost shot two innocent people," the radio blared when we got back into our car.

"That's 10–4, we'll be 10–51," I replied.

Disgustedly the lieutenant said, "I wonder why they need us to handle this?"

"Maybe," I said optimistically, "maybe it won't be as bad as it sounded over the radio. If we can help the man confess what he did and clear his conscience, it will be worth the trip back to the station."

XI. SHE CAME ON STRONG

Neither shall you commit adultery (Deut. 5:18).

If the man almost killed two innocent people, I was thinking as we drove to the station, *then we must be dealing with some kind of sex problem.*

"Loot," I said, trying to break the tension, "sooner or later a man gets caught in his pleasure and the lid blows off. I just imagine the guy waiting for us caught someone 'tampering' with his private property and almost pulled the trigger in his rage."

The lieutenant nodded as he slowed down for an intersection, "Yeah, remember that little nympho we sent you? She almost got shot by her former husband's wife."

I remembered well. I had been called in the middle of the

afternoon by the desk sergeant. They had picked Tammy up as a vagrant and wanted to bring her down to the church office for counsel. Tammy had needed psychiatric help for a problem that bordered on nymphomania.

She was just an average-looking girl—nothing outstanding—in her early twenties. She was dirty and shaggy looking, having spent several nights sleeping on park benches, in unattended automobiles, and with any man who would take her in for the night. Her problem was sex. She couldn't get enough of it!

She blatantly related her sexual escapades with a series of men since arriving in town several days before. Some were bachelors, while others were very much married. When she lacked for male companionship she wandered over to her ex-husband's house looking for him, which irritated his present wife. The new wife had emptied both barrels of the shotgun at her late one night, but even this didn't scare her off. She kept coming back. Her ex-husband was considering taking out a restraining order against Tammy, because his house was starting to resemble a battlefield.

I knew she couldn't keep pestering her former husband and his present wife. I checked with several of her beaus—the eligible ones. They didn't want her. She told me she had been counseled by another local minister who had even offered to give her plane fare back to her hometown. She had refused.

I encouraged her to take the minister's advice and return to her home and her parents. She seemed to recognize her need for help, but harbored an avowed unwillingness to leave our city. Still, she couldn't be allowed to street walk, harass her ex-husband and his family, and run the risk with each affair of contacting venereal disease from some overly willing and unscrupulous male partner.

Our conversation went well into the dinner hour, but I couldn't get her to make a decision. No one wanted her, she had no place to go, and she refused any offer providing her transportation and pocket money to make the trip back home to her parents. I finally suggested she go to a local restaurant for dinner (using a meal ticket our church would provide). I told her I would give her two hours to make up her mind—either to go back home or to go to jail. She agreed to meet me in two hours with her decision.

I really expected she would run out on me. But she was waiting for me when I returned to the office later that evening. However, she had still not made a decision!

We sat in the office glaring at each other. I had the feeling she was defying my offer to help her get home and almost hoping that I'd have her locked up for the night. Neither of us said much; then she leaned forward in the chair and asked, "Well, Reverend, whatcha gonna do? I'm not goin' home, so that means I go to jail, huh?"

She had called my bluff. I knew she didn't think I'd do it, but I couldn't back down at that point. So, away we went, she, quite cooperatively, and I with a conscience that picked at me all the way to the station. It bothered me even more when I filled out the booking sheet and asked her to leave her valuables with the desk sergeant.

I gave her a day and a half and then went back and tried to reason once again. I didn't want to see her spend any more time in jail than necessary. She needed help, and at home she could get it. I took her to one of the interrogation rooms and began my process of pleading all over again. If, I informed her, she would enter a plea of guilty to the vagrancy charge and agree to return to her parents, I believed the judge would suspend her sentence. It worked!

I had contacted her parents and they were willing to have her come back. Her papa had told me how sick his baby was and that he would be eternally grateful if we could get her to come home.

The day of the court hearing, my secretary, Diane, and I sat in the courtroom waiting for the judge to complete the court docket. Her case had purposely been placed last on the docket so it could be handled without others, more particularly the press, being present. The judge listened intently and sympathetically to the circumstances of her arrest, then advised Tammy that she was free to leave—with the understanding she was to return to her parents. She was placed in my custody until she left the city.

Diane found some clothes for her and saw that she was cleaned up. We gave her a good meal, purchased her transportation ticket, and gave her some spending money for the return trip to Minnesota. As we put her on the bus, I apologized for finding it necessary to place her in jail, but believed it was for the best interests of everyone. My parting words were that she should commit her life to God and depend upon Him, believing that He would strengthen and fortify her as she sought the help needed to make her well again.

I really had begun to believe she would make it home. But she didn't. Her "papa" called me four days later and wanted to know where she was. I was stunned. She had jumped from the bus at some station between Fort Myers and Minnesota. I began to wonder if she would find her way back to Fort Myers. She did, all too soon.

She was spotted late one evening, with a male companion, going into one of the downtown hotels. Tammy was back and had her another man. A few days later a local businessman swore out a warrant for her arrest. She had tried to beat a room-and-board bill at his place.

It was beginning to look as if Tammy would never learn. Before she could be located and the warrant served, she was back tormenting her ex-husband. I couldn't do much for her this time, but after she served her time on the petty larceny charge, I determined to make another attempt to save her.

I was waiting for her at the station the day she was released.

We had a long talk about her problem. I told her I wasn't condemning her for her loose living, knowing she wasn't all to blame. She needed help, and the only way to get it was to get back home where it was available. It took another bus trip and another call to "papa," but this time she made it. What I didn't know, though, was that she was pregnant when she left town. She didn't have any idea of who the father was or when it happened. All she knew was that she was pregnant again!

Fortunately, she let God into her life during her second trip to jail. I haven't heard from her since, but I like to believe she got the psychiatric help she needed to find the causes of her nymphomania.

When the Loot and I arrived at the station, at first I couldn't place the nervous man in the lobby, but he knew me. He looked at the lieutenant, then me, and made a mad dash right into my arms—bursting into tears. He was a giant of a man, crying almost uncontrollably. Suddenly I remembered who he was. I had performed his marriage ceremony, and while he and his wife had never joined the church, they were quite regular in their attendance.

I knew Charlie had a very shaky marriage. The foundations were not good to begin with, both parties being on the rebound from recent divorces. I couldn't recall exactly how long they had been married, but knew that I had seen them separately and together several times in the office trying to work out some of their problems. They both drank too much, and he became mean when he overindulged. Charlie's wife, Babe, had had several boyfriends with whom she had been intimate following her divorce and before her marriage to Charlie. *Could she,* I thought, *be cheating on Charlie?* I realized that although I hadn't seen either of them in church for several weeks, Babe had stopped by the office just a few days earlier.

"Reverend Asmuth," Charlie said as he sobbed and clung to

me, "I almost did a terrible thing tonight. I almost did it. I almost killed my Babe and another man."

"I think I understand, Charlie," I said, trying to console him. "Just try to get control of yourself. Everything's going to be all right. The thing is that you didn't do it, Charlie, you didn't do it. You understand? You didn't do it. The gun is there on the desk and not a shot has been fired. Now come over here and tell me what happened."

He was limp and didn't move easily. The lieutenant just stood there, puzzled by what was happening.

"Can you handle him by yourself, Rev?" he asked.

"We'll be all right, Loot," I said. "I've known Charlie a long time, and unless I miss my guess, I know who Babe was bedded down with when Charlie caught them."

Charlie loved to talk, and he started giving me a lengthy and detailed explanation of what had happened.

"You know we've tried, Reverend," Charlie said. "We've come to church on Sunday; we've both been in to see you when things got rough, and we've stuck it out. But something has happened to Babe here lately. She's been acting funny. She hasn't wanted to come to church, and she's been leaving the house at night not telling me where she was going. I began to get suspicious. Oh, I know, I've been doing too much drinking lately and haven't been the best person in the world to live with. But business had been bad, and jobs have been slow coming for me. When I have too much idle time and a lot of worries, I begin to drink, and I've been getting too much."

"What about tonight, Charlie?" I asked. "What happened that caused you to almost kill Babe?"

"Babe told me tonight she was going out for a while; she had some things to pick up at the store, and then wanted to meet one of her girl friends for a couple of drinks at the lounge. I just knew something was up, so I followed her in the other car."

"Did she go where she said she was going, Charlie?" I asked.

"Oh, yeah, she went to the store—you know the one that's open until about two in the morning. She also went to the lounge. I didn't go in. I just sat out in the car and waited. I don't know what went on inside, but I don't think she was in there drinking with her girl friend. Maybe if I had gone in that lounge I might have prevented what almost happened. Anyway, I just sat in the car and waited. I waited for a long time, and then out THEY came. Yes, sir, out THEY came!"

"Out who came?" I found myself asking.

"Why, you know, man. Out came Babe and her old beau, Johnny. Both of them cheating and two-timing on their partners. Why, that Johnny, he's as much married as I am. Anyway, I followed them. They took Babe's car and went directly to Johnny's house. Johnny's wife must be away or else she was out cheating on Johnny. She's done that before, too. I know all about that one."

"I guess you went in Johnny's house, Charlie?" I said.

"Not right away, Reverend," Charlie was saying. "I waited for a while. I didn't know what to do. Then I thought about the gun. The gun was in the glove compartment and it was loaded. I just figured I'd give them both what they had coming. Johnny was a little careless; he forgot to lock the front door when he and Babe went inside. I walked to the house, opened the door, and moved toward the bedroom in the rear. I could hear them carrying on inside that room, laughing and giggling like a couple of school children. Well, it was now or never. I threw the door open, and there they were, going at it. Both of them on that bed, naked as jaybirds without a care in the world, until I kicked that door open.

"Then," he continued, "the fur hit the fan! I flipped a bullet into the chamber and told them they were both dead. Babe, she got hysterical, pleaded with me not to shoot. And Johnny, he just turned white, real white. You couldn't tell where

Johnny ended and the sheet began. Babe's screams did it, Reverend. Her screams did me in. I knew I couldn't pull that trigger. I guess you know some of the names I called her. I just told her to get out, that I didn't ever want to see her again. She jumped off the bed, pulled the sheet around her and ran out the front door. I remember hearing her fire up the engine in the car and heard her take off, but I don't know where she went.

"I just stood there looking at Johnny tremble. Man, he was scared. I had half a notion to pistol whip the guy to death, but he wasn't worth it. I told him that if I ever caught him messing with my wife again he was going to be real dead. Then I left."

"Is that all there is, Charlie?" I asked.

"Yes, sir, I've given it to you straight. What am I going to do now, Preacher? I don't want to lose my woman, but I may have lost her tonight for good."

"I don't think so, Charlie," I said. "You would have lost her permanently had you pulled that trigger. Thank God you didn't go completely berserk. I have a feeling that Babe will be back, but don't look for her at home tonight. I'll bet I hear from her tomorrow, though."

"Reverend, you just don't know how much your being here tonight has helped," Charlie said. "You're my buddy—I want you to know that. You've helped me and Babe a lot before, and I think that between the three of us—and God—we're going to get this thing worked out. I'm just sorry, but then what would you have done if you'd found your wife in bed with another man?"

"I don't know, Charlie," I said. "Perhaps I would've done the same thing you did. One just never knows. I'm thankful, though, that you didn't shoot. You don't know how thankful I am. God be praised for giving you what it took to keep from pulling that trigger."

"There aren't any charges against me, are there, Reverend?" he asked.

"No, Charlie," I said, "there are no charges. You're free to go home. Try to get a good night's rest. One thing, though, I want that gun."

"You just keep that gun, Reverend," Charlie said. "I don't think I have any further use for it."

"One more thing, Charlie," I said; "do you have any more guns at the house?"

"Honest, Reverend, there aren't any more. I took that one off a dead soldier during the Second World War, but you can keep it as a little souvenir of what almost happened tonight."

With Charlie gone and the lieutenant nowhere in sight, I glanced across the lobby of the station to see a forlorn and forsaken young man sitting in a chair holding his head in his hands. There were no personal belongings but a camera case, and the lad wasn't badly dressed. He did, however, give every evidence of a person who had been hitchhiking and for some reason had been brought to the station.

"Sarge," I said, turning to the desk man, "what's the trouble with the boy on the bench?"

"He was picked up because he fit the description of someone we were looking for. But he checked out clean and is free to go. He wants to get back out on the highway but we haven't had a free car to take him to the city line."

Turning to the lad on the bench, I said, "Son, is there anything I can do to help?"

He looked up at me through tired eyes, smiled slightly and said, "Sir, I just want to get home. I don't have but another 150 miles to go, and I want to get home so bad I can't stand it. But I'm so tired I don't think I could walk another mile. I thought if I sat here and rested awhile I'd feel more like hitting that highway again."

He didn't have far to go, but had nothing to do it on. *Well, Rev*, I thought, *that's why YOU'RE here: to help anyone who needs it, and the need is sitting right in front of you. Now do something about it.*

XII. THEY JUST KEEP COMING

He raises up the poor from the dust; he lifts the needy from the ash heap . . . (I Sam. 2:8).

To some unconcerned police officers the lad sitting on the bench was *just another boy*. He wasn't in any trouble, but easily could've been. There was no real tragedy associated with his story. He was simply down on his luck, broke, had lost his job and wanted to get home, yet physical fatigue and exhaustion kept him glued to the bench.

"Son, does a bus ride home sound more appealing than standing on the highway trying to hitch a ride?" I asked.

"Say," he said, looking up, "you're a minister aren't you? Yes, sir, anything would be better at this point than standing on the highway. Do you think you could help me out?"

"We don't have lots of money to use, but since you're only

going to Perry, I think we can hustle up enough change to get the ticket for you. It's partially our fault that you're stranded, so perhaps we can make some of it up," I said.

The boy was no bum. He'd had a job in Key West working for a photographer, but the photographer pulled a disappearing act. Left without funds and no way of collecting the wages that were due him, he was now trying to get home. A northbound bus would be leaving within the hour. The least we could do was help the boy get home.

"Lieutenant," I called, "think we've got time to take this lad to the bus station?"

"Sure, Rev," he said as he entered the lobby. "We'll take him on down. Besides, it'll give us an excuse to finish that cup of coffee we started working on several hours ago. Grab your hat and let's go."

There was just enough time to purchase the boy's ticket, buy him a ready-made sandwich, and put him on the bus. As he started up the steps to the bus he paused and then said to me, "Sir, I'd like to repay you for this ticket and will mail you the money as soon as I get home."

"That won't be necessary, son," I said. "I'm just thankful we could help a little on this last leg of your journey. But here's my calling card. If I can ever help you again, just let me know."

"You just don't know," he said, "how much I appreciate what you've done for me tonight. This is the nicest thing that's ever happened to me in a police station."

"God bless you, my boy," I said as we waved good-bye.

Walking toward the lunch counter the lieutenant said, "Rev, do you do much of what you just did for that boy? How often do you help stranded folks like this?"

"Most ministers in this town have lots of them, Lieutenant," I said, "and there always seems to be a way to get things worked out for people. It's sort of a tangible expression of Christian love. Love in action, I guess you might call it."

Sitting at the lunch counter, we ordered our coffee and continued our conversation.

"Loot, although you always try to help, the big problem is trying to distinguish the cases of genuine need from the frauds and the professional beggars. Some folks just make a habit of going from town to town and church to church, looking for handouts. A few of them make a pretty good living this way. Others really need the compassionate concern of the church in their hour of trial.

"A family with six children phoned the police station one night about eleven. Usually when they stop in or call the station they're on the level. The risk is too great. If they got caught trying to pull the wool over the eyes of a suspecting officer they know they'd soon be behind bars. This family left the lower east coast in a four-wheel rattletrap that was actually being held together with baling wire. Both hood and trunk latch were wired shut. They were squeezed in, with all their earthly possessions, and their fuel tank had gone dry just inside the south city limits.

"This was one of those times when you bend the law a little. The driver didn't have an operator's license, neither did his wife. Their house had caught fire on the east coast; the next morning he lost his job. There was nothing for them to do but head back to Kentucky. What little money they had went for food and gasoline, and both were depleted when they hit town."

"What did you do with them, Rev?" the lieutenant asked.

"I first offered to provide lodging for the night, but they wanted to keep going north. They had a twelve-hundred-mile trip ahead of them, and they wanted to keep moving. They were all hungry, particularly those four growing boys sitting shoulder to shoulder and elbow to elbow in the back seat. We got enough gas to get them to the gas station, and then headed for the hamburger-steak house. I told them to order whatever it was going to take to get everyone filled up. That man and those boys could sure put it away. With everyone fed, I slipped the father some money for the bridge tolls and coffee, knowing that they could get to the Tampa Bay area and perhaps beyond. I also gave him the names of a couple of ministers to the north whom they could contact and who I was sure would help."

"What did you do about the driver's license?" the lieutenant asked.

"We *bent* the *law*, Loot," I said. "Technically the man should have been arrested—no D.L. and no inspection sticker. But, what would you do with him in jail and a wife with six kids on your hands? It was risky, but this was just one of those times when you had to give a guy a break and look the other way. They left town quite happy, completely confident that the Lord was going to find a way for them to get back to Kentucky even though their money and fuel resources would only carry them for the next couple of hundred miles. I'm sure they made it home; people like that always get where they're going."

"Rev," he said, "I don't think you believe anyone is bad, do you?"

"I believe people are basically good. Most of them are the way they are because of bad luck or circumstances. But I've been burned a few times, too, in helping some of these wandering minstrels.

"One called me at home one night and asked if I was the police chaplain. He told me his name, said he was passing through, and wondered if I could get him lodging and food. I told him where to go for a meal, where to go for the hotel room, and then made the arrangements by phone from my home.

"The next morning I got a telephone call from the sheriff's department. It was one of their investigators asking if I knew a certain gentleman. He was the guy I'd put up in the hotel the night before. They asked if I knew where he might be found and I informed them that he was at this particular hotel. I got a shock!

"The call was coming from that hotel. The man was gone, but in the process of leaving he had beaten up a man, taken his wristwatch, wallet, and seventy dollars. The man I took pity on the night before had proven not to be such a good fellow after all!"

"Did that put you out of the hotel business, Rev?" he asked.

"Not completely, Loot," I said, "although it was hard to get room for any single persons for several months after that took place. Thankfully, though, he's the exception and not the rule."

Sipping on my coffee I noticed a Puerto Rican coming into the bus terminal.

"Hey, Loot," I said, "see that man sitting in that corner booth?"

"You know him, too?" he asked.

"No sir," I said, "I don't know him, but a man looking like him came into the office a few days back. He'd been making pretty good tracks in the city. He'd hit the Salvation Army, all the downtown churches, and then came to us and greeted me as if we were long-lost friends. I sat there amazed as he informed me that he wanted a whole new wardrobe. There wasn't anything wrong with the clothes he was wearing, except he was tired of them and wanted a change. He then proceeded to tell me that we were pretty poorly equipped in this city to take care of his kind and that we should be better prepared to handle those who were looking for handouts.

"I told him I would not buy a bus ticket, nor would I give him a complete change of clothes. I did, however, offer him a meal. When I set a $1.50 limit on the meal he called me 'cheap' and said that the least I could do was give him a $3.50 limit!"

"You're just too good sometimes to people, Rev," the lieutenant said. "They're going to take you for all they can get. I've seen them put the touch on you and you just can't seem to say no. How come?"

"What's a fellow going to do, Loot?" I asked. "You've got to help when the need is there. You remember that boy they arrested just a few days ago—possession of stolen property, improper tags, no driver's license and a couple of more things? He is still serving time in jail. The girl with him, though, was just along for the ride. She ended up sitting in the lobby of the station with nothing but the clothes on her back. You tried to call her folks in Oklahoma collect, and they were so poor they couldn't even accept the charges. I got that one, too."

"Yeah," he said, "I heard that the girls in records all chipped in and bought her a couple of meals, and you gave her a bus ticket back to Oklahoma. I guess she was pretty happy when she learned that a way had been found for her to return home."

"She was a pretty happy little girl, Loot," I said smiling. "It would've done your heart good to see the expression of gratitude on that girl's face when she boarded that bus. Now don't get me wrong. She wasn't an angel. She was married, but was traveling and living with this other man. But, then, who am I to prejudge someone else? You learn to take things one step at a time. The first step with this girl was to get her back home. Some would say that you're just transferring your problem to someone else. Yet she didn't want to stay in our area so it seemed best to show compassion in the way that seemed most meaningful and relevant at the moment."

"That's an interesting philosophy you've got there, Rev," the lieutenant replied. "Say, whatever became of our Louie? I haven't seen him in a long time."

"The day he was released from jail someone sent him to me. There aren't too many guys who have any money when they're released. If they had money they'd get themselves out and not serve the time. Louie had just run out of money. He had a place to stay, but needed some groceries, and had to have a prescription filled. I bought Louie a few days' groceries, some cigarettes, and got his prescription filled. What I didn't know was that Louie had a lot of prescriptions to be filled. He was going to every druggist in town with a prescription for this and a prescription for that, telling the pharmacist to send me the bill.

"It hit me about the first of the month when the bills started coming in. Louie further complicated things by putting in for repeated grocery orders. He'd come by and say that on Monday he had a job and would be going to work, but the Monday that he was to start his job never came. We wised up to each other about the same time. I think Louie sensed I was about to blow the whistle and call the MAN on him and that was the last I ever saw of Louie. But he did have a good thing going for him while it lasted. He got so brazen during the peak of his 'begging' that if he couldn't find me at the office he'd call the police station and tell them to locate me."

Coffee time was up and we leisurely walked from the bus terminal to our cruiser, looking nonchalantly at some of the characters seated about the bus terminal.

"You know, Loot," I said, picking up the conversation again, "there's a difference between the person or family that is destitute and the professional beggars we get throughout the year. I know I shouldn't give in, but even with the 'pros' I find it hard to turn them down."

"You've always responded whenever we've had to call you

with one of these cases, Rev," the lieutenant said. "I can't recall a single instance where you've been unable or unwilling when the boys at the station have needed you."

"These are the often sad cases that call for a contemporary and practical demonstration of Jesus' Parable of the Good Samaritan, Lieutenant," I said. "This is really what it's all about with these cases of human need. Often a constructive deed, done in love, means more than any words that we could speak or prayers that we could offer. In a way, you're expressing your prayer, perhaps not verbally, but in a gesture that reflects the witness of Christ's Church, at a time when a guy is down and about to be kicked in the teeth again."

"I guess if I understand you, Rev," the lieutenant said, "it's that you can't get a man's attention on an empty stomach. That you can sometimes reach a man faster by a deed of kindness and mercy than you can by speaking words. Do I read you right?"

"You sure do, sir," I replied. "And if the church and her people fail in ministering to their neighbor—*anyone in need*—then the church has failed. You've known me long enough to know that I'm not a goody-two-shoes. I don't go around with a long face, a black suit, and a Bible tucked under each arm. Yet I've tried to act in these situations in a manner that is in keeping with the ethics of my calling in Christ, and in a way that the person in need can sense the genuine concern of a Christian who is ministering in the name of Jesus Christ."

"I've a long way to go, Rev," the lieutenant said. "I once thought I could bring you down to my ways, but slowly you're bringing me up to yours. Keep at it long enough and you're going to make Christians of all the policemen."

"I can't make Christians of them, Lieutenant," I said, "but you never know at what point or at what moment God is going to reach out and touch their lives and make them into new creatures. God has His ways and His times. And you're not really as bad as you like to make me think you are. Underneath that external tough-policeman veneer is a real person. I've seen you in a lot of situations and I know you're good."

He couldn't say much after that, and we just rode through the quiet streets of the city wondering what would happen next.

XIII. THE SHOOT-OUT

You shall not kill (Deut. 5:17).

"Fort Myers to cars four and fifteen," came the crisp, cold call. The cars answered in sequence.

"Cars four and fifteen go to 43 Ivy Terrace. Some sort of a family disturbance."

We headed in the direction of the complaint, but somehow we turned on a wrong street and were momentarily lost.

"Lieutenant, I just heard a shot!" I blurted out. "Somebody's shooting a gun, right over there!"

When the lieutenant decides to stop a car, he stops it! WOW! It's a wonder I didn't suffer from whiplash, but he didn't stop seconds too soon.

Six older teenage boys came running up out of the drainage ditch and fell prone directly in front of the police car. I jumped out of the car, flashlight in hand.

"Have you guys lost your marbles?" the Loot said. "What's the big idea?"

One of the six, obviously badly shaken, stammered and stuttered, "There—there's b-b-been a shooting over there." He pointed shakily into the darkness.

"That's no reason to lie down in the middle of the road," said the lieutenant.

"But—but—" replied the boy, "I—I thinks they is still shootin' it out!"

He was right—they were! There were four more shots in rapid succession, and we found ourselves flat on the pavement beside the boys. My imagination visualized the headlines:

"Police lieutenant and chaplain still missing in action!"

We couldn't see, but we could hear the guns banging away in the still night air. The shots were followed by a strange, pained moaning. Then nothing but stark silence.

The boys related what had happened, and directed us to the scene. It wasn't far, but it was dark! We gave the dispatcher our location, Musket Alley, and drove down a spooky row of darkened shacks looking for the victim of the shooting. A gun fight, yet there wasn't a solitary soul in sight, and not the first light burning.

We moved through the area with extreme caution, my adrenalin pumping feverishly. One of our flashlights hit an old junk car farther down the alley with one door open.

"Lieutenant," I barely whispered, "what about that old junk car? Could someone be in it?"

He instructed me to crouch up against one of the shacks, while he—with gun drawn—cautiously and slowly moved toward the car.

"Now you be careful, Rev," he said softly. "I don't want either of us shot dead tonight, and if this Yo-Yo has shot one, he'll more than likely shoot again rather than run the risk of being caught."

Like a preying lion about to jump its victim, the lieutenant eased toward the junk car. Reaching the car he rose slowly until his eyes met the bottom of the rear windowpane. Then his flashlight searched and he called for me.

I ran the few remaining steps. When I reached the car I saw a man slumped over in the back seat, lying in a pool of blood. We attempted to find the pulse. There was none! A bullet in the back of the head, one in the shoulder, and two in the back. He was dead—shot four times from behind.

"You know what to do now, Bob," the lieutenant said.

"Yes, sir," I said, turning to leave and get on the car radio.

"Car four to Fort Myers. We've got a signal 5 (murder). Send a detective, ambulance, and the coroner. And dispatch two more cars so we can search the area for the assailant."

The shacks were all raised a couple of feet off the ground, resting on cement blocks. The killer could be under any one of the buildings; he could be in the darkened areas between any of the houses; or he could be in one of them.

Almost as if on signal, lights started coming on and people started gathering. Minutes before, it was so forsaken and quiet that only an occasional croak from a bullfrog broke the silence. I could hear the hushed whispers of the gathering crowds. The morbidly curious approached the car, gasped at the horror scene and walked away. No one knew anything, or if they did, they weren't going to tell—at least not yet.

In between two of the buildings, I heard the sounds of labored breathing. Moving closer, I spotted two small boys, sobbing and trembling with fear. As I approached them I identified myself and questioned them ever so gently. I suggested that they come to the car with me; we could talk there, and no one would bother us. Reluctantly, they tagged along, then sat beside me on the front seat of the cruiser, fascinated by all the activity on the police radio.

By now another car with uniformed men was on the scene,

and the detectives and ambulance had arrived. All that was missing was the coroner. The detectives, I noticed, had found what was apparently the murder weapon, a rifle, in the trunk of the car.

One of the boys beside me was shaking with fright. "That man will shoot us, too," he said. "He's in that building over there. He's got a gun and he's going to kill us."

I relayed this information to some of the officers and they began a search of the shack while the boys continued to talk.

"Boys," I said, trying to reassure them, "no one's going to hurt you. You're safe, and you can help us find that bad man if you will just tell me what you saw and what you heard."

"Well," stammered one, "Luke, the man who was shot, was having this argument with Big Joe. They were arguin' over Big Joe's woman. Big Joe told Luke to keep his hands off his girl. Luke said she wasn't Big Joe's girl, that she was *his* girl. They just got louder and louder. Then they started pushin' each other 'round and wrestled on the ground. Luke got up and started runnin' toward the house near the end of the alley. But, he just wasn't fast enough."

"Yeah," said the younger of the pair. "Big Joe ran crazylike to his car, gets his shootin' gun out, and there's a big loud bang! Luke just took a couple more steps and fell to the ground. When the gun went off, we ran. We were scared, Mister Policeman, we sure were scared."

That was easy to understand. "Did you boys see anything else?" I asked.

"No, sir," said the younger boy. "We just took off and ran. And we stayed in hiding until you spotted us between those buildings."

They were able to give me a description of what Big Joe looked like and what he was wearing. This information was quickly relayed to the other officers searching the area for the assailant.

"Boys, you just sit here in this car," I told them. "Don't leave; don't talk to anyone. You just listen to what's happening on that police radio."

I maneuvered my way through the crowd of morbid onlookers, trying to catch bits and snatches of the conversations. Half of the hundred or so spectators were drunk. They were chock-full of speculation and eager to pass it on to anyone who would listen. But it was all hunches, no real information.

Shoving his way through the crowd was a tall, well-dressed man. Crying and angry, he headed straight for the junk car. Someone said he was the dead man's brother! At the sight of his brother's bullet-ridden body he screamed out and collapsed in my arms. A bystander helped me drag him to a nearby porch step.

It was another sad hour. He started hurling abuses at God, cursed the man who had killed his brother, and vowed immediate revenge.

I identified myself to a bystander and said, "I don't know where this man lives, but I'd like you to help me get him away from the crowd and to his home."

He nodded in agreement. I don't know how far we walked, but we passed through row after row of dilapidated old shacks, dodged yesterday's laundry hanging from clotheslines, and stopped abruptly when a rat jumped from a garbage can and scurried beneath the building alongside. I learned in our long walk that the man's name was Willie.

We reached Willie's apartment, literally dragging him most of the way. The apartment was entered through the kitchen door, and upon flicking on the light I saw the cockroaches scatter in all directions. We took Willie to his bedroom and placed his enormous frame on the bed.

He'd rambled almost constantly. Not everything he said was intelligible, nor was it nice.

Okay, Rev, make your religion come alive to a guy at a time like this. You've got a tiger on your hands and you'd better realize it, I thought.

"Willie," I said, placing my hand firmly on his shoulder, "I'm the Reverend Asmuth. I'm going to stay with you awhile. And Willie, you and I are going to talk. We're going to talk about a lot of things—about you, about Luke, about your God, and about—"

Willie raised up abruptly on the bed, shoving me to one side, and lunged toward the drawer of his bureau. "Reverend," he said, with fierce intensity, "I'm going to talk—I'm going to talk with this gun right here in my drawer. And I'm going to talk to Big Joe like he talked to my brother—with real bullets."

Man, I thought, *this guy's desperate. Now I've got to talk him out of a gun and not get a bullet in my head in the process.*

"Willie, you aren't going to kill Big Joe!" I said with all the authority I could muster. "Come over here and sit down for a minute before you do something that's going to get *you* in real trouble, too," I commanded.

He obeyed.

"Now, Willie, put that gun on the nightstand by the bed. I'm not going to try to take it; I just want you to put it down on the table."

Like a man hypnotized, he followed my second order!

We were eyeball to eyeball now. I stared him down and told him, "Willie, two wrongs don't make a right. We've got several police officers here right now searching the entire area. Their job is to find your brother's killer. And when they find him, Big Joe will go to jail and be tried in the courtroom and be punished for his crime. But understand, Willie, you can't take the law into your own hands." I paused, wondering if any of it was sinking into his mind.

"You mean exactly what you said, don't you, Reverend?" he questioned.

"Yes, Willie, I do. On the wall I see a picture of Jesus standing at the closed door. Over there I see the Twenty-third Psalm. If you and I read the same Bible it says, 'Love your enemies,' and again, 'Blessed are you when men revile you and persecute you . . .' Look, Willie. God isn't responsible for what happened tonight. He didn't kill Luke, and you can't go through life blaming Him for what took place. He didn't do it. Two grown men got into an argument over a woman. Both had too much to drink, a fight began, and a gun was fired. Man's foolishness and sinfulness caused your brother's death—it wasn't done by God."

It was kind of tough for Willie to fathom all this, upset as he was, but I was beginning to get through. He was much calmer now, and sobbing very little. I continued:

"God is concerned with how you handle this tragedy and what you do with your life now that this has happened. Luke's gone. But you've got to go on, go on for a long time."

"You're startin' to make real good sense, Reverend," Willie said. "It really wasn't God's fault that Luke died tonight. It was too much cheap whiskey and an evil woman. She wasn't good for Luke, that woman. She was a bad woman. God has got to help me pull through this bad thing that has happened. But I'm sure if I pray to Him, pray long and hard enough, I'll get the help I need and the answers to my questions."

"I know you will, Willie, I just know you will," was my response.

Things were beginning to look better, and I felt I could safely leave Willie's home. His friend assured me he would stay with him, and I convinced Willie the safest place for that revolver was back in the bureau drawer. He put it there, just as I suggested, which completely amazed me. He was calming down now, and the biggest favor Willie's friend could do was to try to get him to sleep. I knew his perspective would be different in the morning. The grief would still be there, but maybe more of the bitterness would have subsided.

I was about to excuse myself, when I had another thought. "Willie, look closely at that picture of Jesus on the wall. I want you to go to bed now and get some rest. Lying on your bed think of the One who is the Good Shepherd, the One in that picture. Remember, too, how He said, 'Peace I leave with you. My peace I give. Not as the world gives, give I unto you. Let not your heart be troubled, neither let it be afraid.' Think deeply on that."

His hand reached out and grasped mine firmly. "Thank you, Reverend. You've been kind and helpful. Good night."

"Good night, Willie, and God bless you." I turned, passed through the kitchen, and out the door.

The detectives were now dusting the car for fingerprints, and the uniformed men had searched the area with great thoroughness in a futile attempt to find the assailant. One of the neighbors knew Big Joe's full name, and where he might be headed. By now an all-points bulletin had been put out on the suspect, and things were under control.

I had almost forgotten about the two little boys whom I'd ordered to remain in the cruiser until I returned. They were still waiting! Their eyes were as big as saucers and dancing with excitement. The activity on the radio held them spellbound all the time I was away. Although I had made some notes on their story, I felt it would be best if they could relate what they saw to one of the detectives. They were really the best witnesses we had for this case.

One of the plainclothesmen came over to the car. In a fatherly way he joked and kidded with the boys. They loosened up and began joking back with him, and then excitedly shared their story.

The coroner had come while I was gone; the dead man had been removed, and only a smattering of people remained on the scene. They were either suffering from insomnia or just didn't want to miss anything.

"How're you doing, Rev?" the lieutenant said.

"Loot, I think that I'm coming along just fine," I answered. "But this place is beginning to give me the creeps. I keep thinking any minute that killer's going to jump out of the bushes and put a slug in one of us."

"Yeah, we're about finished, Rev. Let's go."

The plainclothesmen still had some things to do, but they were able to take care of themselves, and didn't need any assistance from us. My two little friends had also disappeared. I never even got around to thanking them for all of their help. Oh well, they'd be able to read about it in the papers the next day and then get scared all over again.

XIV. THE UNEXPECTED

Woe is me because of my hurt! My wound is grievous (Jer. 10:19).

You gradually learn in police work that you are to expect the unexpected. There is a phrase in the Bible that speaks of "not knowing what a day or a night will bring forth." Law enforcement is like that. When you receive a complaint or an assignment you have a limited amount of time in which to prepare and make some predetermination of alternatives you will follow when you arrive at the scene. Thus, even if it's bad, you are psychologically prepared for what might follow. The unexpected that you happen to stumble upon can often be unnerving. It's then that your conditioned reflexes are sharply brought into focus.

But, expected or unexpected, one eventually becomes calloused and at times hardened. One inwardly trembles at the sight of the first drunk, physically shakes when initiated into a barroom brawl, and becomes sick at the sight of blood and violent death. You learn from experience, however, and it is sometimes easier the second time around. Yet in every situation there is always the element of something new.

I was coming off the bridge on the north side of the river one afternoon when I noticed a great deal of activity down by the riverbank. I spotted three police cruisers, a fire truck, and Chief Underhill's car. I knew it had to be something out of the ordinary because the Chief was there.

I eased my car down to the riverbank. Several small boats were dragging the river in the immediate area of a large dredge. The fire department was standing by with resuscitating equipment, and several curious onlookers were lined along the bank of the river.

The Chief motioned me over to his car and quickly shared what he knew. A teenage boy, a member of a dredging crew, had accidentally fallen overboard. He disappeared in the twenty-foot channel and had been under about fifteen minutes. The Chief indicated he thought a young boy standing by the river's edge was the victim's brother.

One look at the boy and I knew he must be kin to the drowned boy. He was standing by himself, tears streaming down his cheeks, murmuring softly, "Why, God? Why did it have to be Benny?"

He had witnessed the entire incident. Now he was standing there watching the boats drag the river for his brother's body. I introduced myself and put a fatherly arm around him, offering my help.

"Just don't leave me, at least not for a few minutes," the boy said. "I want you here by my side."

"Would you like to come sit in the car?" I asked. "There isn't much we can do now except wait."

"No, sir," he replied. "If you don't mind I'd just like to stand here. I can't leave until they find my brother."

We watched and waited. The boats moved back and forth in the area around the dredge, dragging constantly. The Police Underwater Operations Unit was now in the water with its divers, but they were hampered by the murkiness of the water. The operation could take a long time, but I knew the boy was not leaving until his brother's body had been recovered from the river.

One of the boats looked as if it had hooked onto something. Turning to the boy I said, "I believe they've located your brother."

He turned his gaze to the boat several yards away from the dredge as the waterlogged, lifeless body was pulled from the water. The boy watched the boat with the dead victim disappear under the bridge pilings and head for the city docks.

"My brother," he said haltingly, "he's dead, isn't he? He's been in the water too long and now he's dead!"

"I wish it could be otherwise, but you're right," I answered sadly.

The lad shook his head in disbelief. "You know," he said, "my brother didn't have to die. We were supposed to wear life vests. But he got careless about his and didn't have it on when the accident happened. What I don't understand is how he went down so quickly. He was an excellent swimmer. If only he had worn that life vest." He paused, then continued, "Sir, I want you to take me over there."

"Over where?" I asked.

"You have a car, don't you?" he replied. "I want to go over to that dock where they're taking my brother. I want to be there when they take him off the boat. I've just got to see him again. Will you do it, sir? Please?"

"Come on, son," I said, "let's get going or the boat will beat us."

The two of us left the scene of the drowning and moved into the flow of traffic in the southbound lane of the bridge. My traveling companion rode along in silence, and I didn't want to force him to talk. Perhaps it was best that he was alone with his own private and inner thoughts.

When we reached the city docks, there were police cars, sheriff's cars, an ambulance, and the coroner waiting. The boat was still several yards offshore when we walked onto the dock. People react mysteriously when standing in the presence of death, and no one spoke.

"Reverend," the boy said softly, "where will they take my brother when the boat comes?"

"I don't really know, son," I answered. "It depends upon the coroner's inquest. He may ask for an autopsy, or he may just release the body to a funeral home. We'll just have to await his decision once the boat arrives."

"You won't leave me, will you? At least not for a while? I'm going to need your help, I just know I am," he said.

The rescue squad, now approaching the dock, eased the boat gently into its berth. The ambulance crew was standing by, and the body was lifted from the boat and placed on a waiting stretcher. The coroner performed his duty with professional precision, and indicated an autopsy would not be required. It was death by drowning, with no suspicion of foul play. A clean white sheet was placed over the body and the funeral home attendants pulled the stretcher toward the hearse while the lad and I followed. As the stretcher was about to be placed in the ambulance the boy spoke again.

"Sir," he said turning to me, "I'd just like to see my brother again before they take him away. Ask the men if they will take the sheet off so I can see him just once more."

The men from the funeral home looked at me skeptically, but I indicated it would be all right to grant the lad his request. He had been quite brave throughout the ordeal and seemed to be man enough to take what he was about to go through. The sheet was lifted back.

The boy stood in a cold, stony silence, then dropped to his knees, placed his head upon his brother's chest, and began crying uncontrollably. It had been building up in him, and the floodgates had to open so he could get it all out. I knelt at the boy's side realizing he was showing a normal grief reaction and it was best to let him get it out of his system. Almost as abruptly as he started crying, he stopped. A calm, peaceful look came on his face and he said, "I'm going to be okay, now. I'm going to be okay."

"Let's get back to the car; we've got a few decisions to make," I said.

We watched the ambulance leave the city docks and head in the direction of the funeral home, then walked in silence back to the car.

We sat in the car talking, and I learned that the boy, whose name was Kevin, was from a small community in southern Ohio. He, his brother, and his father had worked on river dredges on the Ohio River. They were now living with their stepmother, and their father was also employed by the dredging company. His father also had witnessed the accident.

"Where is your dad now?" I asked him. "Do you have any idea at all of where he could be?"

"I don't know where he is," Kevin said bitterly; "he just walked away. He stood there with me on the shoreline for a few minutes watching 'em drag the bottom; then he just walked away. I don't know where he went. He just said, 'Kevin, you take care of things.'" He paused, then asked, "Reverend, do you think we could go to the funeral home? I've got to begin making arrangements for my brother's funeral."

"Don't you want to wait until later in the day? Perhaps you'd like to talk with your dad and stepmother before doing anything," I said.

"No, Reverend," Kevin replied. "I know my dad's upset and really can't think clearly. That's why he just walked away. I know that whatever I do will be fine with the family. Just your being here has meant so much to me. We haven't been here long enough to make any friends, and you don't have any free time on a dredging job. You know that dredge just works away twenty-four hours a day, seven days a week. And we work those seven days a week also. There just isn't any time left over. I haven't even been to church since I left Ohio several months ago."

"Kevin, I'll stay with you just as long as you need me, and help you in any way I can," I said as we drove to the funeral home.

The funeral director was on hand when we arrived, and was extremely helpful in an awkward situation. Kevin wanted his brother's body shipped back to Ohio. His mother was up there along with a large number of immediate relatives. The funeral would be held in the church, with burial in the family plot in the cemetery on the churchgrounds. The casket selection was made, clothing discussed, travel arrangements for him, his dad, and stepmother all worked out to everyone's satisfaction. Not a single detail was overlooked.

"I've taken care of everything that I should take care of here, Reverend, so I guess we can go," Kevin said. "I don't have a car, and I stay way out in the south end of the county. Do you think that you could take me home now?"

I nodded and we started on our way, the boy directing me where to turn. "What will you do when this is all over, Kevin?" I asked. "Do you want to come back to Fort Myers, or will you remain in Ohio with your mother?"

"Oh, I'll come back," he said. "The company will give me the time that I need for the funeral and handling any personal affairs afterward, but I'll be back. This is the only work I know, and one day I'm going to have my own dredging company and crew. There's always going to be a big demand for dredging."

It helped Kevin to have someone who was willing to respond naturally in a time of need. God was using me to minister to a child of His at a crucial moment in this boy's life. Neither of us had known each other a couple of hours before, but I felt now as if we knew each other quite well.

"Keep praying for the strength you're going to require for the events that still lie ahead of you," I told him. "Just give God an open heart. He'll go with you and help you. He will make a difference."

That was the last I ever saw of him. I returned to the river's edge where it had all happened. I just sat there looking at the water. I was emotionally and mentally drained and exhausted. Over and over again, I kept saying, "Why, God? Why did this terrible thing have to happen to this boy?" The sun was setting. It was the prettiest time of the day on the water, and the river looked so placid and peaceful. The water looked quite harmless. The only sounds were from the passing cars on the bridge and the mournful, monotonous groaning of the dredge which was now back in operation. It was almost as if nothing had happened, as if it were all a bad dream. It was a moment that brought back all the tragedies I'd seen since I'd worked with peace officers. The terrible things paraded before me by the river's shoreline late that day and I seemed to recall all the details of all of them.

No matter how much tragedy you've seen, and no matter how gruesome, it never fails to touch you because you never become completely insensitive to it. When you lose your sense of feeling and ability to identify with the guy who has a real shattering and traumatic mishap, you lose an essential ingredient in life.

Sometimes it's difficult to go to sleep after a night in the prowl car or an afternoon at the hospital. The worst episode I ever experienced, without a doubt, involved a little two-year-old boy. The station called me at the office and said a small child had been struck by a speeding car. They wanted me to get to the emergency room of the hospital as fast as I could.

I lost no time making the trip and pulled in seconds after the ambulance did. The child had been a beautiful boy, with blue eyes, shiny blond hair, and a deep Florida tan. He was now a lifeless mangled mess. He never knew what hit him as he darted between two cars and into the street.

I'd seen lots of accidents, shootings, knifings, and bloody violent deaths. But this one was different. It put things back in their proper perspective. This one didn't have to happen. The driver was traveling too fast for conditions.

I realized that it could have been my son who was lying on that blood-soaked stretcher. And as I walked from the emergency room to the lobby to break the news to the boy's parents, God and I were having a heart-to-heart talk with each other. I don't remember all that went on between us, but I kept saying over and over, "God forbid that I should ever become so hard and calloused that I can't feel the other man's pain and share the other man's grief. Help me to know what he's going through that I might better minister to him in Your Name."

I believe God helped me as I tried to help that family through that loss of the boy. When I returned home later that day, my bouncing and bubbling blue-eyed blond two-year-old was waiting at the door. That was my undoing. I grabbed that fellow in my arms, clutched him so tightly that I thought he would break, and then came unglued at the seams. I just clung to him and cried like a baby. Never before had I reacted that way, but I was so torn up inside when I realized that it could have been my John on the stretcher, that I went all to pieces. I've never forgotten the chain of events of that day. That single incident, a long time ago, has preserved my humaneness and hopefully enabled me to be compassionate and consoling when another has walked "through the valley of the shadow of death."

Sometimes the lieutenant says, "I'm sure glad we have you around on some of our tough cases, Rev. You're so much better geared to handle some of this than we are. I'm not at all sure that I'd know what to say or even how to say it. It's so much easier for us just to have 'the Rev' do it."

But words don't come easy when someone has experienced a death, especially if it's under abnormal or tragic circumstances. And sometimes words don't mean a great deal. It's your presence that counts. Symbolically, a minister represents God to a lot of people. His very presence seems to convey the assurance that God is standing by their side. What many don't know, however, is that God would stand by their side whether the minister was there or not. We simply provide the medium in many cases through which this takes place. I don't think I ever feel any greater sense of inadequacy than when I'm with folks who have been visited by the angel of death. Yet I know that my presence is helpful and has pulled a lot of people through some bad scenes. God, in a strange, mysterious, marvelous, and often miraculous way, uses me as His instrument. I simply commit myself to Him in all things, place my trust in His unfailing providence and care, knowing that He will guide me and cause me to do what is right.

XV. HUMOR AND PATHOS

Rejoice with those who rejoice, weep with those who weep (Rom. 12:15).

I often stop by the station on my way home from a meeting at the church in the evening. I can't even recall why I dropped in one particular night. The eleven-to-seven-shift lieutenant was on vacation, and the sergeant was in charge of the officers on duty. He wanted me to ride awhile and I did.

There wasn't any activity. Everything was quiet, and we had a leisurely cup of coffee at one of the all-night spots before driving around some more. We parked the car near the front entrance of a cocktail lounge and just watched happy people come and go.

Then a girl appeared from out of nowhere. She was wearing a sleeveless blouse with a deep scoop at the bosom exposing a large portion of her mid-section, and she had on skin-tight, hip-hugging slacks that played peekaboo down the outside of both legs. She walked over to the car, rested both arms on the window ledge and poked her head in on my side. She batted her eyes and said, "Whatcha doin' tonight, honey?" Obviously she didn't know who I was since I was wearing street clothes, nor had she seen the sergeant sitting opposite me in his uniform.

Just as she was about to move in for the kill, she detected the sergeant. Swish!! She just disappeared. Vanished. We looked around but she was just not to be found. I was red-faced and embarrassed, but the sergeant found it hilarious. He doubled up with deep belly laughs and had tears running down his face. It took me weeks to recover, and I never will live down the kidding I got from the boys at the station.

Riding the patrol cars is often humorous. One night we received a complaint that some boys were stealing hubcaps from cars in one of the plush neighborhoods. An unmarked car was dispatched into the area in an attempt to spot the boys. We were driving down a dimly lit street and suddenly saw three boys run from one side to the other. We stopped and jumped out, but they continued running. The lieutenant shouted at them, and suddenly I heard something whizzing through space. I ducked, and not a minute too soon. One of the largest grapefruit I've ever seen caught the upper doorframe of the car. Splat! Grapefruit, seeds, and sticky juice were all over everything, especially me. Had I not ducked when I did, I would have caught the thing right in my face. As it was, I was sticky for the rest of the night.

When the boys saw the lieutenant and realized they'd hit a police car, they stopped and slowly walked toward us. I heard one little shaver in the group blurt out, "Oh, no! Reverend Asmuth! Now I really *am* in trouble."

The lecture began. They were not the boys stealing hubcaps. They were camping out for the night, and decided it would be fun to toss grapefruit at passing motorists. They had, unfortunately, chosen the wrong motorist!

I knew all of the boys. They were really good kids and were just being a little mischievous. But they were in hot water and the one fellow from my church just knew he was going to spend the night in jail. We impressed them with the seriousness of what they had done and suggested they get back to their camping and leave the passing motorists alone. Terry, the boy from my flock, said, "Mr. Asmuth, you won't tell my folks about this, will you?"

"I promise that this will remain just between the two of us," I said solemnly, raising my right hand.

"I have a feeling, Rev, that you've saved a few young ones in your day from being carried down to the station," the lieutenant said as we got back in the car.

"You're right, Loot," I answered. "I hate like the mischief to see a kid get dragged in and have a juvenile citation issued when a little fatherly admonition and a stern rebuke alongside the road is all that's necessary. It doesn't always work, but in many cases it does. The kid will often think more highly of the lawman and be inclined to regard him as a friend rather than as the guy who is simply out to bust him and have him tossed in jail."

There was another night when we were quite busy. I was riding with the shift lieutenant as I normally do. We were called to answer a complaint. When we arrived at the scene, a deserted parking lot, one of the detectives came over and asked if I could go with him on a special detail. Obviously the lieutenant wasn't aware I had left the car, for moments later he left the car also, accidentally leaving the car in reverse. He was talking with his men and noticed the cruiser going around in circles in the parking lot of the shopping center, in REVERSE.

"What's that crazy Reverend doing, running that car backward in circles out there?" he said in amazement to one of the patrolmen.

"Lieutenant, the Reverend went with the detective. I think you left it in reverse," the officer said.

Even though I wasn't to blame for that one, the boys still chuckle about the Loot trying to blame the Rev for his mistake.

Another incident involved a couple of young female schoolteachers who were renting a house in a nice neighborhood. There were a lot of trees in the yard, and the house had a noisy metal roof—the kind where if an acorn hits it you think someone has dropped a cement block on it. These girls had been frightened badly by someone who was running around on the roof, trying, they were certain, to get into the house. Three cars responded to the complaint and I was in one of them. We could hear whoever it was up on the roof, and assured the girls that we would catch him. We surrounded the house, with a man on each side, while whoever was on the roof kept running from one side to another.

Someone said, "If he jumps off your side, Rev, don't let him get away. Just yell for help and we'll back you up."

There I stood, billy club in one hand and the flashlight in the other, just knowing that the prowler on the roof was going to jump right into my arms.

"Rev, he's coming your way! Don't let him get away!" I heard him coming and shined my light up on the roof, moving it from one side to the other. Suddenly I detected two closely set eyes.

"Hey, men!" I shouted. "I've got your prowler. Come quick!"

The men all moved to my side of the house. There on the edge of the roof was their prowler—one of the prettiest raccoons I'd ever seen.

One of the advantages of being a police chaplain is the large number of fans you collect among the younger set, many of whom I've met through talking in the schools about the drug problem.

We had a disturbance complaint one night involving a couple of hundred teenagers. They were all on their way home from a dance, and some kind of a misunderstanding developed between a couple of the boys over a girl. When we arrived we couldn't even get down the street with the cruiser. It was lined with kids filling the block from one end to the other. The lieutenant got out and I tried, but just as I was about to open my door about twenty boys moved in on me.

As they approached the car, ganglike, one of the boys said, "Hey, I know you—you're the Rev."

"Yeah," another cried out, "he's the Rev. He's our friend. He ain't gonna let them put nobody in jail cause HE likes us."

I had less confidence in my abilities with that gang than they did, but they were sure I'd get everything worked out. One of them darted off and disappeared in the crowd, but was soon back with the two boys who were having the disagreement.

"Now, you just listen to the Reverend," he told them, "and everything will be okay."

We stood around having a little rap session, while most of the other kids moved on out. I talked with the boys and suggested they shake hands and set aside their differences.

"See, I told you, man," my anonymous friend said, "the Rev can take care of anything."

We picked up two boys one night on a stolen car charge. They were juveniles, and hadn't really conceived of their act as theft. They had just "borrowed" the car, and had planned to return it. The problem was that the owner discovered the theft, reported it, and it became a stolen vehicle since he was going to press charges. When the boys were being booked and charged they realized that they were in trouble. Then their worries began.

The trauma of it hit when they were informed that they would be released in the custody of their parents, and they had to call home. If they refused to make the call, we would make it for them, but the call had to be made. One boy completed his call and advised us that his folks would be down very shortly. He knew he was in trouble in more ways than one. The other boy reached his parents, but it was a fiasco.

This lad told his mother he was in bad trouble, that he was at the police station and she should come down and pick him up. She refused to believe him, saying he was playing a joke. The arresting officer then got on one phone, and I got on the other. We both pleaded with this woman, trying to make her understand that her son was at the police station and in serious trouble. The woman hung up on us saying that the patrolman was not a police officer, I was not a Reverend, and her son was not in any trouble with the law. Furthermore, she informed us, she didn't have time for such childish jokes and pranks.

We made a believer out of her, though; we sent a car to the house a few minutes later and firmly advised her she was to come to the police station as fast as she could get there.

I can still see one little girl about seventeen who was brought in with about five other teenagers one night. They all knew what they had done, were guilty, but didn't want to accept the fact that an arrest had been made. They were all of an age where they could be jailed with no questions asked if they were unable to make bond.

One by one the kids called home with varying results. Some parents were horrified and appalled, some were downright mad, and some refused to come, saying the kids could spend the night in jail. Then the seventeen-year-old got on the phone.

She started extolling her virtues to her mother, sharing the great injustice that had happened to her. Her closing remarks were, "Mama, now you listen to me. You get yourself down to this police station just as fast as you can. Do you understand, Mama? I want you down here right now, and I want you to straighten the hell out of them!"

She got away with it. If I had ever talked that way to my mother or dad I'd have been bounced around the room like a rubber ball. Thank God, somewhere along the line I was taught to have respect for authority.

Many of our current problems stem from the utter lack of respect for authority so many kids have today. They get away with it at home, they get away with it at school, and they think they should get away with it with the police. We're seeing more and more of it all the time. And when I see how some of the parents conduct themselves when they come down to the station to pick up one of their kids, I'm not surprised at the behavior of the children. It's as if parents have adopted the philosophy of spare the rod and spoil the child.

Besides that, some parents are teaching their kids to become pretty good liars. We picked up a sixteen-year-old boy one night for illegal possession of alcoholic beverages. The partially consumed glass was sitting beside him in the car, and his breath was a dead giveaway. He was quite frank about how he had been able to get the liquor, what he had been drinking, and how much. It seemed a shame to bust him since he'd been so cooperative and honest with us. It was his dad and his employer who blew the whole thing.

The father came storming down to the station and in a very belligerent fashion informed us that his son would never be guilty of illegal possession of anything. His boy was a paragon of virtue. When we showed the father the half-empty glass, he put the blame on someone else. It just had to be the boy riding in the car with his son. As it happened, the boy's passenger was clean; he hadn't touched a drop. We had already released him and sent him home, yet the father stood there trying to deny the whole episode. The boy's employer was called in at the request of the father, and he, too, insisted that such a thing could not have happened.

It wasn't until we started getting static from the dad and the employer that we placed the boy under arrest. We had originally intended to bring him in, call the parents, and have an honest talk about the seriousness of the problem. We might have done better that night if we had booked the kid's dad and employer. They were causing the scene. In effect, they were telling the boy that it was all right to lie, even when caught in the act. Just deny it. Whatever you do, don't tell the truth.

I made the mistake of asking the boy where he went to church. His father answered that one, too. "We don't go to church. We can't be bothered hanging around with a bunch of hypocrites. I'm plenty good as I am, and I don't want any church telling me what I should and should not do."

In his answer I detected some of the cause of the problem. Too many people today have cast aside religion, because they feel that they are sufficient unto themselves.

Respect begins with a respect for the Almighty. It goes from there into every facet of life. From this respect for God comes something else, a deep and abiding personal relationship with Him. It is this relationship we develop that then proceeds to give us those sound moral and spiritual values upon which great lives are built. God's Word becomes real and meaningful, and we abide by it. His teachings and His commandments become the basis upon which we make our decisions and order our lives.

I see it every day, but see it more when I ride with the men each week. People are living empty and purposeless lives, because they have not found God. So many of them don't feel needed or wanted, and their satisfaction comes from booze, sex, or violent acts of crime. They're just walking empty shells that live and breathe.

I remember a drunk who tried to kill himself by jumping off the bridge. Only his relaxed drunken state kept him from being killed when he hit the water. I learned, after we got him dried out, that his wife had left him, his family had disowned him, and since he couldn't seem to breathe a sober breath, his employer had let him go. In spite of what he had done and tried to do, I thought he was worth trying to salvage and knew that God could do it. God did do it. It took a lot of courage on the part of this man, and the temptation to revert to his former ways kept tugging away at him. But he stuck with it. He hasn't touched a drop since the night he jumped—four years ago. Now he's back with his wife and doing exceptionally well in the business world.

I know it was God who changed that man. God had always been some kind of a remote Being to him, Someone who was very unreal all of this man's life. He had heard Him talked about, mostly abusively, but sometimes in a reverent way, yet God meant nothing to him until he almost drew his last breath. It was then that he realized everything else had failed, and God was all he had left. He flung open the doors of his heart and gave God a chance; the difference was miraculous.

His pocket New Testament was a source of strength when the days were hard and the nights were lonely. The church, which before was a hollow ritual, was now a sanctuary to which he could retire and become refreshed and fortified for the struggles that awaited him in the outside world. God helped him stick with it.

I know this in a very personal sort of way. I shut God out for a long time and as a result was one of the meanest men around. I could talk as well as some of those other cussers we've had in that booking room, and was steadily going from bad to worse. But I found that God had other plans for my life and was going to win out in the end. When I accepted Christ, my world changed. I became a happy person and saw things in other people that I'd never seen before. Things like the golden rule meant something, and the teachings of the scriptures that had held little meaning for so many years suddenly became plus factors in my life.

Today, I feel if I can add just one brick to the wall of human dignity, then what I am trying to do is worthwhile and has eternal significance in the Kingdom of God.

XVI. THIEVES IN THE NIGHT

Neither shall you steal (Deut. 5:19).

The streets were deserted and the city was mostly asleep! The newspaper delivery boys were out on their routes, and the milk and bakery trucks had started their predawn deliveries. Even the drunks had found places to lay their heads, and it was looking as if the frenzied pace of the past several hours was at an end. Strange how the moving hands on the clock seem to change the complexion of the city.

The lieutenant and I found an all-night eating spot without any customers and went inside. It was a nice feeling, having a restaurant all to ourselves with no one to bother us. We had a refuge!

Sleepy as I was beginning to get, I needed the black coffee. It looked and smelled good. I knew I couldn't hold up much longer, and the coffee was going to become the stimulant I needed to get me through what remained of a very long night. The lieutenant sat reading a newspaper while I indulged in reverie, letting my mind drift back to a time two days before Christmas.

We had a report of a prowler in an automobile junkyard, and a couple of cars were sent to investigate. Walking through one of those places in the dark is hard on shins! We combed every inch of the place, but found nothing. It was when we started walking back to the cars that we spotted an old junker parked down the road, about a quarter of a mile from the yard itself. Cautiously we approached the car and found a middle-aged gentleman sound asleep in the back seat.

Before waking him, we hurriedly checked out the car with our flashlights and discovered a collection of hubcaps, wheels, tires, batteries, and several other odds and ends. The owner of the junkyard was with us and was positive these automotive parts were stolen from his yard.

The man wasn't the least bit disturbed at being awakened and politely answered all of our questions. He couldn't understand what all the fuss was about. He said he was working north of the city. A friend had given these items to him and he was waiting for the yard to open so he could sell them. He was going to use the money to buy Christmas presents for his family.

He gave himself away when he volunteered to unload all the stuff there on the side of the road if we would let him head on home to his wife and family. We held him for further questioning.

A records check revealed he was a convicted felon out on parole. He was in big trouble, and by the time we got him to the station he knew it. He had violated his parole on several counts, and he was going to be sent back directly to the State Penitentiary to complete the terms of his original sentence.

It sounded like a time of confession when he called me aside in the station.

"Reverend," he said in a voice choked with emotion, "I did steal those things from that junkyard, and there's no sense in lying about it. All I wanted to do was get a little money so I could buy Christmas presents for my wife and children. I just can't explain why I lifted those things."

He wasn't the only one who couldn't understand it. The man had quite a bit of money in his pocket, enough to buy nice Christmas gifts for his wife and children; yet he elected for some unknown reason to steal again.

"Sir, I know I don't have any right to ask a favor because of what I've just done; but do you think I could be allowed to spend Christmas with my family?"

Judges are human and tend to be forgiving and tender-hearted at holiday times, but this was an impossible request. I felt for him and knew what being home at Christmas meant, but there was just no way. The only hope we had was to stall until after Christmas. It was not likely that the prison bus would be coming through town to make pickups the day before Christmas. I knew he couldn't go home, but we might just be able to detain him in our jail until after the holidays. At least his family could come and spend Christmas with him in our cellblock. It wasn't the best deal, but it was better than not seeing or being with them at all.

The probation and parole officer went along with my suggestion the following morning, and we kept the man as our guest in the city jail until after the holidays. His family spent the day with him, and although he was returned to Raiford a few days later, he left with a good attitude toward what was facing him for the next couple of years. He did not have the bitterness toward the police and our judicial system that surely would have been there had we acted otherwise. This is the kind of love the world shares and knows at Christmas when God's love for us becomes real in the Babe of Bethlehem.

Sometimes I'm accused of being partial to the bad guys. I'm not. I just want to see that they get a fair shake. One of society's real problems is that of accepting those who have served their time in a correctional institution. These people have paid their debt; they've lost their rights and privileges; and they're asking for a chance to make a new beginning.

Yet, tragically, we encourage them to revert to their former ways. We don't want our young people associating with them because they're BAD! We don't welcome them into the life of our churches because they're supposedly not as good as we are. They find so often complete and total rejection, that SOCIETY forces them back into doing the only thing they know —a life of crime. With a lot of these criminals, we helped create the monster in the beginning that led them to their criminal acts. But the real sin is our unwillingness to take a chance and to give someone else a chance to prove himself. You can't do what is right and become what you want to become unless someone is willing to take a few risks.

I've been down this road with boys before, and know the problem from firsthand experience. We once had a boy who was fleet-footed and developed a good bit of expertise in the field of burglary. Like most of them, though, he tripped himself up and was caught. He was almost shot in the process. I knew him as a boy with wonderful possibilities before his life of crime began. Rejection caused it. He was rejected by his parents and found no love or affection or understanding at home. His friends at school rejected him, and mothers were leary of letting their daughters be seen in his company. It didn't take too long before he got the message. He wasn't wanted! Crime inevitably followed.

He was caught, tried, convicted, and sentenced to two years

in the state prison. He was faithful in corresponding with me while serving his time, and I tried to keep him buoyed up. He was eligible for parole at the end of fifteen months, provided we could get him employment. I promised to help him. Yet he had to spend another forty-five days in the state prison because we couldn't find anyone who was willing to give him a chance. Jobs were plentiful, but I made contact upon contact only to have doors shut in my face.

"He's a jailbird," they said, "and we don't have any room for jailbirds in our business." Tragic, because these were responsible and leading citizens in the community who said, "No, I can't take a chance!"

It seemed futile. Why bother getting him out if he doesn't have a chance to mend his ways when he comes back? A man can be rejected only so long before taking up again the only profession he knows.

Finally, through the kindness of an old Roman Catholic friend in the construction business, we worked out a deal for the boy. It worked beautifully. We discussed his returning to the community with his family. The boy needed love now more than he had needed it at any time in his life. They had to find a way to give it to him. I invited him to church because life isn't much without God. Some of the church folks were skeptical about having a convict worshiping in the congregation. But I explained that the way to keep him from becoming a convict again was by taking his hand and showing him the way through love.

It required great community effort and resolve, but the boy was restored to a normal life. It can be done, but only when each of us sees that we have some personal responsibility in assisting in the rehabilitation process.

"You know," the lieutenant said, looking up from his paper with a twinkle in his eye, "you never seem to give up even though the going gets rough." It was as though he had sensed what I had been thinking. "What's important to me is your sense of conviction, believing as you do that everyone, no matter how bad he has become, can be redeemed and restored. This is almost more than I can fathom. It's unreal."

"Jesus didn't think so, Loot," I said somewhat sternly. "He believed in the worth of a person. Matthew was a tax collector and in many ways a real con man because he took far more than he should have taken. But Jesus saw something good in Matthew and he became one of the twelve disciples. Zacchaeus was another tax man, bilking his subjects, but Jesus changed his ways, too.

"We just underestimate God. We're unwilling to believe He can do all He is capable of doing. But when we believe with every fiber of our being in the power and the ability of God, all things are possible."

The lieutenant was at a loss for words, which was unusual for him because he could always come up with something. At least he was thinking, and maybe he was coming closer to my way of thinking than he wanted to believe or realize.

"Maybe to prove my point, Loot, I should tell you about a particular boy . . ."

Larry was in his early teens, had a brilliant mind, was well liked and did exceptionally well in school. Yet he wasn't loved, nor did he feel wanted at home. To get his parents' attention he built up an impressive list of breakings and enterings. He masterminded each move very carefully, and never left any clue since the mode of operation was different with each act committed.

The sole clue was the type of robbery. It was always a sporting-goods store or a bait and tackle shop. And it wasn't wholesale robbery of these establishments either. The merchandise was always discreetly chosen, and he never emptied out any one establishment. This continued for about a year and a half and had the criminal investigators completely baffled. He even managed to return to some places twice, but caution and selectivity were always his bywords.

He tripped himself up one day by going to one of these shops to exchange a piece of equipment. The proprietor became suspicious since it didn't seem likely that a boy this young could afford the piece of equipment he brought to the store. The store owner's stalling made the beads of sweat break out on the lad. He knew he was caught. He didn't resist or deny. None of the merchandise he had stolen had ever been used, and it was all returned to the original owners.

It was a matter for the juvenile authorities, and he faced the grim prospect of being placed in one of the boys' correctional schools in the state. During the lengthy interrogation process, he kept referring to his feeling of rejection at home. His acts of thievery were simply the means he had employed to startle his parents. He kept hoping with each theft that he would be caught, and probably he became intentionally careless, which led to his arrest.

He was released in the custody of his parents until the hearing before the juvenile judge could be arranged. One day his mother called me. She could endure almost anything, she said, but could not bear the thought of her son being placed in a boys' home. I agreed to discuss her son's case with the juvenile authorities but could not make any promises because the decision rested with the judge. In return I asked her to do one thing.

"When was the last time you put your arms around that boy and gave him a real indication of how much you do love him?" I asked. There was nothing but silence on the other end of the phone, and I was beginning to think that she had hung up on me.

"Don't you think I love my son?" she finally asked.

"I don't know, ma'am," I answered. "I simply said that you've got to *express* your love for the boy. You've told *me* about it, but I don't matter. He's the one that's important. He committed those crimes because he wanted the attention and the love of his mother and dad. If he means all you've said he does, you folks better begin right now to find concrete ways to express it."

"That was all it took, Loot. Hitting her verbally with the cold facts of the matter became the turning point in that boy's life. I kept my promise and discussed the entire case with the juvenile people. He received a stiff period of probation, but there was no sentence. That family became a unit instead of three people living in isolation in the same house. A kid went straight not because he feared the authorities or was running the risk of being sent away, but because he began to feel wanted and needed in his own family. Today he's a well-adjusted young man who's going to go places in the world. You see, Loot, he wasn't a bad boy, but became temporarily bad simply because he thought nobody loved him."

"Did religion play a part in this one, too, Rev?" the lieutenant asked. "Where did God fit in?"

"It was God who made the transformation possible. They were relatively good church people, but this was a situation that was going to put their convictions to the test. It meant that they were going to have to put the love of God that they had read, sung, and heard about into tangible expressions in their day-to-day relationships with each other," I said. "It worked. It always works when we take God at His word. I've never known Him to fail yet."

XVII. IT WAS JUST A DOG

For which is the greater, one who sits at a table, or one who serves? (Luke 22:27).

To the person passing by in the dark of the night we were just a couple of police officers standing on the side of the road getting ready to stomp on someone and put them behind the bars. But to those of us who were there and witnessed what took place, it was a sentimental scene of the lovable and affectionate cop. No brutality, nothing but gentleness from one who cared.

It was just a dog! A furry little mongrel that was a child's pet had been struck by a passing automobile. The motorist had stopped, but because it was late he didn't know what to do. Few cars were on the road at that time, and he was hovering over the dog when we drove up.

"I just didn't see him crossing the road," the man said apologetically. "I don't know if there is anything we can do for him.

A child somewhere is going to be mighty upset come morning when he finds that little dog is gone. If you do find the owner, I can make things right and buy the child another puppy."

The uniformed officer took a second look at the dog and realized he was not dead. He bent over him and with skilled hands searched the dog's body for signs of broken bones or open wounds.

Looking up he said, "Rev, radio the station and ask them to call the animal hospital and tell them we're bringing an injured dog out to them. They might also try to find the vet. This dog doesn't have to die."

"Will do, sir," I said as I returned to the car.

When I returned to the scene, the patrolman was trying to place his hands under the dog's body so that he could lift him off the pavement and carry him to the car without worsening his injuries. While he worked, he was speaking softly to the little animal, assuring the dog that everything would be fine. No one could have been treated more regally than the pup as he was lifted from the pavement and placed on the back seat of the squad car for his ride to the animal hospital.

The story wasn't front-page news; it never made the blotter at the station. It was just one of the many gestures of goodwill that the patrolmen perform a thousand times over every working week. No one ever hears about them, but they happen every day.

Another one that never made the blotter involved the group of kids from out of town who were in Fort Myers attending a dance one night. When the dance broke up and they got ready to leave, they discovered that someone had stolen their distributor cap. They walked to the station and asked if there was anything we could do to help.

Automotive supply stores are not open at 2:00 A.M., and

distributor caps for foreign automobiles are not stock items in the few all-night service stations we have in the city. The kids had a problem and we tried to help.

The dispatcher put a car on the detail—to search for a distributor cap for a particular make and model foreign car. When he exhausted the resources that were available at that hour of the morning, he advised the station of the futility of his mission.

Then the deskman picked up the search by telephone, trying contacts he knew of that might conceivably either have a distributor cap or know where one might be found. The boys on the shift wanted to help. After waking up several people, we located a man who had one in his shop. This merchant got out of bed about 3:00 A.M., went to his business establishment, and then came by the police station with the needed part to make the young people's car run again. It was probably a three dollar item, and it cost considerably more than that if you compound the man hours devoted to locating it.

One of the cruisers picked up the young folks at the station, drove them to their stranded vehicle, and assisted with the installation of the new part. An officer stayed with those kids until the car was running, and they were on their way home.

There are times, however, when you just can't be the good guy forever. I've been in on some of them, too. One night we were called to the parking lot of one of the banks shortly after the bars had closed. There was a lot of commotion and noise. Two young couples in the group had spent the bulk of the evening in the lounge drinking and dancing. They were trying to get a car started—without keys! The driver had lost the keys during the evening, and this little gang was trying to hot-wire the car to get it going. Their progress was nil. They were doing too much feuding and fussing among themselves to achieve their purpose. We were not welcomed with open arms, but we sensed their need for help. The lieutenant and I both knew a little about wiring and asked to have a look. We emptied the car of passengers and then crawled onto the dirty floorboard to try to wire the switch.

In his panic the driver had clipped the wiring harness so close to the terminals that splicing was impossible. Both of us spent almost forty-five minutes trying to put the thing back together while three of the kids searched the area for the keys. The driver stayed with us, severely criticizing us for our slowness in what he had completely failed to do.

The kid's lip finally got the best of us. Nothing we did was right, and we were just a bunch of dumb lousy cops because we didn't have that car running for him. There we were, flat on our backs underneath the dashboard of his car trying to get the thing running, while he was breathing down our necks, calling us a couple of bad apples.

The lieutenant poked his head out from beneath the dash and said to the boy, "Cool it, man, or you'll find out how lousy we really are." He had taken about all the lip he was going to take from this boy for one night. We worked several more minutes but knew it was going to take an ignition man to get the car running again.

Crawling out of the car and brushing the dirt off of each other we tried to politely tell the boy that the car wasn't going anywhere for the rest of the night. He pitched a fit, and at the same time we determined his destiny for the remainder of the night. We had been willing—up to that point—to provide transportation for the kids and see them all safely home. He spoiled it for everyone.

He was placed under arrest and put in the back seat of the car. We sent the others on their way in a taxi. We checked with the town to the north where he was from and learned that he had taken the car without his father's permission. This explained why he was so up-tight when we couldn't get it going. His dad said the boy could just spend the night in jail and he'd be down for both the car and the boy in the morning.

The police blotter doesn't tell the full story of most incidents. No mention was ever made on the log sheet of the night we were called out on a noisy party complaint. Two cruisers responded. There were kids all over the house when we arrived. They ranged from fourteen to twenty-two years of age. They were on the floor, the couches, the beds, under the beds, in the closets—they were everywhere. And there was beer all over the place.

When we walked through that door they rose like soldiers ordered to attention, arranging their clothes which were mostly in a state of disarray. We had the goods on every one of them, and I've never heard such begging and pleading in all my life. Two things they didn't want. None of them wanted to go to jail, and none of them wanted us to call their parents.

Many of the girls were on the verge of hysterics, and the boys knew their school careers were shattered if they were taken in and booked. I knew many of these kids, and there had to be a better answer than jail. Yet they had to be punished in some way for their bad behavior and have impressed upon them that the legal drinking age in this state is still twenty-one.

We had an idea we thought would work. We gathered the army of kids together in the living room. First, we lectured them on the wrongness of what they had done. Next, we lined them up, gave them each a can of the unopened beer, told them to pull off the flip top, and then marched them to the kitchen sink. One by one they emptied their opened can of beer and watched the contents go down the drain. The process continued until we had emptied every can of beer in the house.

We've never had any more trouble with any of them since that episode. We spared them embarrassment and jeopardy to their schooling and careers, and we won some friends. Another good deed by a bunch of cops.

Another incident took place when we received a complaint that there was a noisy pool party going on at a high school at 1:00 A.M. The pool was surrounded by a high wall, and it was difficult to find an opening where we could look on the inside. When we did find a peephole, we couldn't see anything. At last we positioned ourselves where we could get a general view of the entire pool area. Through the darkness we detected two people, diving, swimming, splashing, and carrying on without a care in the world. We put an end to their fun and games by turning on our powerful flashlights. The beams picked out two naked boys in the water.

"Police!" the lieutenant shouted.

I kept my light on the boys while the lieutenant ran to the other side of the pool area and waited for the boys to climb over the wall.

We could have booked them on a variety of charges: swimming in an unguarded pool, illegally using school property, violation of curfew. But they were just being boys.

We talked with them and found they were spending the night together. They just wanted to have a swim before they went to sleep. We returned them to the boy's home where they were staying, advised them not to leave again, and went on our way. The boys, with tears in their eyes, thanked us profusely and thought that policemen weren't as bad as everyone said they were.

One night one of our young officers picked up a fifteen-year-old girl for questioning. She was tall, slender, and rather attractive with long black hair. She was dressed all in black—sloppy longsleeved top, bell-bottom slacks, and dirty bare feet. The officer said she was smelly, as if she hadn't had a bath for some time. She was totally uncommunicative when arrested for vagrancy under the name "refused" and placed in the cell-block.

It bothered the young officer that the girl was locked up. He went back to the compound and brought her into the interrogation room, determined he was going to get through to her. Most of the men on his shift had gone at eleven that night, but he and another stayed and tried to communicate with the girl. Nothing seemed to break through the wall between them. She stared into space for the longest time and refused to even give her name.

After some behind-the-scenes detective work, one of the officers came into the room with a piece of paper bearing the girl's name. It was then that she broke. If we knew who she was, it wasn't going to be too hard for us to find out where she was from and send her back. As it developed, her life had been spent in foster homes and orphanages. She just went from one to the other, and was now living with a family she didn't like in the Tampa Bay area.

Her mother had died when she was five, and she had not seen her father since. She was a ward of the court, and ten years of foster homes and orphanages were beginning to show. Eight days earlier she had run. Her nights had been spent sleeping on park benches, on the beach, and in unlocked and unattended automobiles. Three days were spent sleeping and smoking pot with four men at one time, but they tired of her and kicked her out.

She told the officers they might just as well get it over with and send her back to Tampa. But they knew this was not the solution to the problem the girl was facing. She wanted help, but seemed unwilling to accept it. They had a distinct feeling that she couldn't trust anyone, that she had been taught to hate the PIGS. What she didn't realize was that these PIGS were different.

The arresting officer checked with his wife and the shift lieutenant. It was satisfactory to release the girl to the custody of the one officer and his wife for the weekend. Monday would allow contacts to be made in Tampa. Then they could see what the possibilities were for keeping the girl with a family in Fort Myers. It amazed the girl when she found police officers wanting to be of help.

She had second thoughts about the whole thing sometime over the weekend and ran, trying to get the officer's daughter to go with her and take the family car as part of the deal. The girl may still be running, since we've never heard anything further on her. But here again is a case of human need where officers responded not because they had to but because they wanted to help someone who seemed pathetically helpless by herself.

It had been a long night and I was picking up my gear from the front desk—notepad, flashlight, and billy club. My billy club! *Billy club,* I thought, *you've been a constant companion through the years. You look as if you've fought many battles judging from the nicks and scratches up one side and down the other. But you've never hit or hurt anyone and I hope you never do.*

"Kind of attached to that stick, aren't you, Rev?" the desk sergeant said, interrupting my thoughts.

"Sarge, I've had this stick a long time," I said. "We've been through a lot together, but I want to believe that it has all been good. Maybe, by the grace of God, we can keep our record clean so I can keep my billy club as a traveling companion that never has to be used to inflict harm or bodily injury upon another. That's the way I'd like to keep it."

"Finally decided to call it a night, did you, Rev?" Mr. Gorrell asked. "If you've been going all day and all night too, I can just imagine how weary you must be. I'll sign you off duty and hope you'll be back."

"I'll be back, Mr. Gorrell, you know I will," I said, "and you also know where to find me if you need me before then. It has been a long night for me, and I'm headed for home!"

Just as I was leaving the station I heard the lieutenant calling, "Rev, hold it a second, will you?"

He appeared in the lobby and stood by me in the doorway. "I've been thinking," he said. "We've kidded a lot with each other, but would it be all right if I came to church on Sunday? Maybe come and bring my family with me? I'm not sure I'd know what to do, but if you think it would be all right, I'd like to come."

"Be all right, Lieutenant?" I said excitedly. "I'd be pleased as punch to have you come. You know you're welcome. This has been the best news I've heard all night. The Loot is coming to church! I'm going to hold you to it now." Then, half-jokingly, I added, "And don't worry, Loot, the building is strong enough to take it—see you Sunday."

XVIII. NOW I KNOW WHY

For the Son of man also came not to be served but to serve (Mark 10:45).

There was something that could be described as a good-all-over feeling as I walked to my car parked behind the station. The early morning air was clear and fresh, and the eastern sky had a low-key pink glow as the sun was about to make its morning debut. The night for me was over, and I drove joyfully toward home and bed. The night lights of the city disappeared behind me as I crossed the bridge and headed out into the country for the short drive to the parsonage. It had been another dirty night's work and part of the dirty job of being police chaplain. What tragedy I'd seen, and what unhappiness and loneliness I'd witnessed in the long night behind me. Yet, I was compensated and rewarded in a number of ways.

The people the officers and I encountered throughout the night were the kinds of people for whom Christ died. They were the people He was identified with during His ministry, and of whom He said, ". . . those who are well have no need of a physician, but those who are sick. Go and learn what this means, 'I desire mercy, and not sacrifice.' For I came not to call the righteous, but sinners." If ever a person was surrounded with the dregs of society it was my Lord of whom it was said, "this man receives sinners and eats with them." The greatest justification for doing the work of a police chaplain is the life and ministry of Jesus Christ. In Him you will find the ministry of One whose life was devoted and whose message was directed to the downtrodden, the outcasts, the forsaken, the lonely, and the lost.

In one of His parables Jesus told the story of the man who had a hundred sheep. The herdsman lost one and left the other ninety-nine to go after the one which was lost until he found it. Then says the Master of men, "I tell you there will be more joy in heaven over one sinner who repents than over ninety and nine just persons who need no repentance."

The lost coin and the lost son tell the same story. There is always joy "before the angels of God over one sinner who repents."

Parading before you on the streets of the city under the cover of darkness are the people whom Jesus spoke about, the ones who are lost and the ones whom the church has failed to reach. We've failed to reach them because the church hasn't thought they were her concern. Down through the ages organized religion and the institutional church have been breathlessly busy and panting about many things. Our time has been consumed in creating ecclesiastical organizations, structures, powerhouses, elaborate programs, and issuing decrees and pronouncements as if mere words held the saving power of the Risen Lord of life! Our time has been taken with building programs to enable us to have facilities in keeping with our desires and our financial resources. And, to the outsider, to the empty and hollow souls whose hearts cry out for the living God, we've said, "You're not welcome. You're not good enough for us." Spiritually starved, neglected masses of humanity pass by our doors and we feed them not!

The time has come to drop from our foam-rubber cushions of comfort to the hard floor of humility and say again, "If

Christ died for me, He died for you too. If He is seeking those who are sick and those who are lost, then I must join Him in this ministry and in this search. I must join Him in His ministry of love, and compassion, and concern." There's no other answer.

We may be able to say at the end of the day, "I've kept all Thy commandments, I've observed all the 'thou shalts' and the 'thou shalt nots.' " Yes, we may be able to say it and feel good about it, but we can never sleep with a clear conscience at night as long as we know that in our waking moments there have been injustices we have not tried to correct, human hurts we have not offered to bind up, and masses of God's children who long for the saving knowledge of Jesus Christ to whom we have failed to tell the Good News.

In our personal Christian growth we've got a long way to go before we can say to the woman living in sin and standing at the well, "Neither do I condemn you; go, and do not sin again." So many of us would be the ones to cast the first stone, not realizing that there, but by the grace of God, go I! God must touch our hardened and calloused hearts and continue to touch them until we realize that we are to be a "light" to ALL people, and not just to our friends and those whom we like and choose to associate with in life.

Being a police chaplain is a valid and meaningful ministry to me. It removes me from the isolated and insulated ivory tower of the local church out into the marketplace where people live, where people sin, and where people die. It helps me understand these people and be sympathetic to them and with them. But it has also made me a better minister to my own flock. I can appreciate their dilemmas and conflicts, and help them wrestle with their problems because I know from firsthand knowledge on the street the things of which they so often speak. When you've seen with your own eyes and heard with your own ears, you don't sit in righteous judgment upon one of your own church family. You know the torment and the living hell they have been subjected to and are now experiencing. You know, too, that Jesus wasn't just uttering pious religious phrases but was speaking the great truths of the centuries that would abide forever, truths that in and of themselves when applied to our daily living, relationships, and problems make the difference between abundant life and death.

Now I know why I'm out on those streets week after week exercising an often lonely form of ministry. God has called me to do it, and I have responded. But it isn't a ministry for everyone, and not all are well suited for it. It requires nerves of steel, a stomach strong enough to stand violence and bloodshed, a mind that isn't easily shocked by terrible obscenities, the courage to know that out there on the front line where the action is, a bullet or an assailant's knife could have *your name* on it, and the ability to let the power of your convictions stand firm in the face of frequent temptations.

While all can't do *this,* we have not been excused by God from ministry to humanity. When Jesus said to us, "Go therefore and make disciples of all nations," no one was excluded. The Bible speaks of "varieties of gifts," and "varieties of service, but the same Lord; and there are varieties of working, but it is the same God who inspires them all in everyone. To each is given the manifestation of the Spirit for the common good . . . All these are inspired by one and the same Spirit, who apportions to each one individually as He wills." Inability to serve in one capacity does not excuse us by God from serving in another. God expects each of us to respond to human need in a way that is unique to us.

Across the length and breadth of this land, however, there is a need for those who care and can stand it to consider this as an extension of their ministry in the community in an area where it is surely needed and will be appreciated. Here you will meet some of the sorriest and most neglected specimens of humanity ever to roam the earth. You will see them at their worst, and attempt by God's grace to bring them to their best and finest. Here you will work with police officers who lead lonely and often misunderstood lives. You will be permitted to stand by them in their finest and often most courageous hours. And you will have one of the richest ministries in terms of personal satisfaction you can ever know. This may not be your "bag," but if it is, there is a law enforcement agency right now who would be willing to have *you* on *their* team. The Apostle Paul said, "let a man examine himself," and this ministry with police officers asks just that. If you think you've got what it takes, can tolerate the many inconveniences you will be subjected to, and want to do something truly worthwhile, volunteer your services today.

The church or its agent must be present in every known arena of life. Why not extend your ministry to this one? When the judgment day comes, God is going to judge each of us by our genuine response to human need. When God says, "Whom shall I send. Who will go for Me?" perhaps you can answer by saying, "Here am I, send me."

Epilogue

Why should YOU do it? Because Jesus said:

"When the Son of man comes in his glory, and all the angels with him, then he will sit on his glorious throne. Before him will be gathered all the nations, and he will separate them one from another as a shepherd separates the sheep from the goats, and he will place the sheep at his right hand, but the goats at the left. Then the King will say to those at his right hand, 'Come, O blessed of my Father, inherit the kingdom prepared for you from the foundation of the world; for I was hungry and you gave me food, I was thirsty and you gave me drink, I was a stranger and you welcomed me, I was naked and you clothed me, I was sick and you visited me, I was in prison and you came to me.' Then the righteous will answer him, 'Lord, when did we see thee hungry and feed thee, or thirsty and give thee drink? And when did we see thee a stranger and welcome thee, or naked and clothe thee? And when did we see thee sick or in prison and visit thee?' And the King will answer them, 'Truly, I say to you, as you did it to one of the least of these my brethren, you did it to me' " (Matt. 25:31–40 RSV).

This, you see, is what it's all about!

Information on the police chaplaincy may be obtained by writing to:

The Rev. Robert C. Asmuth
P. O. Box 1356
Fort Myers, Florida 33902

THE ASMUTH FAMILY

REVIEWING WANTED POSTERS

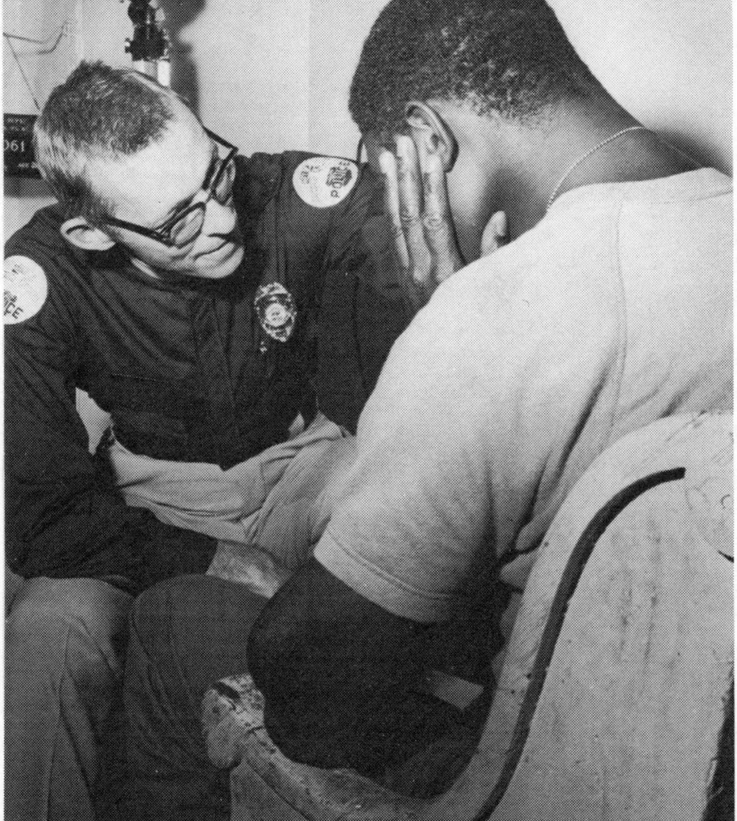

A PRISONER CONFIDES IN REV

WORDS OF COMFORT TO THE DISTRESSED

REMOVING A CAR FROM SCENE OF AN ACCIDENT

VIOLET AND BOB ASMUTH